D1552241

Foreward

This book is a probing into a single art form—puppetry—and how that art form can be integrated into the life of the Special Child in establishing and expanding a multi-sensory learning experience. Although this book is written with the disabled as its primary focus, the concepts are adaptable to all children. In a sense, all children sustain a handicap when cut off from the potential richness of education, for education as a whole is taught on a one-dimensional plane, rather than as a multi-sensory experience. It is only through the introduction of ideas that challenge young minds with techniques that are attention compelling and innovative and invite active participation that a heightened sense of learning can be achieved.

The work represented throughout this book reflects the attitudes and experiences of people who see learning as an enrichment to the individual, an experience to be enjoyed by both teacher and child alike. Because of their diverse backgrounds, their specific approaches may differ, but their goals are in sync with one another, as they reach out and seek ways to experiment with the new. Puppetry, here, serves as our model, but it is hoped that this book, both in its conceptualization and its spirit, will inspire similar explorations into other art forms to help expand the world of the learning child, both special and other.

Nancy Renfro

Presenting the works of

- Cynthia Roup Harp
- Judith Schwab
- Texas School for the Deaf-Library
  Claudia Leonesia
- Hutchinson Sunflower Puppeteers
- The Underground Railway Theater
  Debra Wise, John Lewandowski
  and Wes Sanders

WITHDRAWN
BALDWIN PUBLIC LIBRARY

Nancy Renfro Studios
Austin, Texas

SEP – 9 1986 B. & TAYLOR

To My Mother
Helen
Who Gave Me Encouragement

Other Books published by Nancy Renfro Studios
Puppetry in Education Series

PUPPET CORNER IN EVERY LIBRARY
PUPPETRY AND THE ART OF STORY CREATION
PUPPETRY AND CREATIVE DRAMATICS IN STORYTELLING
PUPPETRY AND EARLY CHILDHOOD EDUCATION
MAKE AMAZING PUPPETS (Learning Works)
PUPPET SHOWS MADE EASY!
POCKETFUL OF PUPPETS (Series)
(Can be obtained from address below)

Copyright © 1984 Nancy Renfro
all rights reserved

The author, however, grants permission for patterns and drawings shown in this book to be reproduced by the individual teacher for use in **non-profit** puppet activities in the classroom, church, library, theater or recreational areas. No part of this publication may be reproduced or transmitted in any form or means (electronic, mechanical, photocopying, recording or by an information storage or retrieval system) for any other purpose without the written permission from Nancy Renfro Studios.

ISBN 0-931044-12-X

Published in the United States of America by
Nancy Renfro Studios 1117 W. 9th Street, Austin, Texas 78703

Cover Credit
Front: Magic Fairy Bodi-Puppet/Cynthia Roup Harp Project
Back Top: Underground Railway Project/photo by Lorenzo Deitch
Back Bottom: *Puppetry and Imagination Project* by Judith Schwab/Photo by Jim Carter

Photographs taken by Nancy Renfro or Debbie Sullivan unless noted otherwise
Illustrations by Nancy Renfro

Acknowledgments

Innumerous people were involved in the creation of this book over the span of several years. My collaborations with sensitive artists and teachers who care deeply for the creative potentials of the disabled child have been truly joyous ventures. The work of Cynthia Roup Harp, Judy Schwab, Claudia Leonesio and the Hutchinson Sunflower Puppeteers and Debra Wise, John Lewandowski, and Wes Sanders of the Underground Railway Puppet Theater are highlighted in the manuscript. Repha Buckman and Edward Pazzanese I graciously thank for initiating and writing articles included in this book.

I wish to thank the Texas School for the Deaf and staff members who generously allowed me to innovate and try out ideas as well as photograph projects in action with the children. It was on this campus that the seeds for this book were planted.

Various other individuals, photographers and groups also contributed to the book's success and are acknowledged within each chapter. Their energy and effort are noteworthy.

I want to give a special thanks to my long term friend, chief editor and consultant Ann Weiss Schwalb whose constant support and advice have buoyed me through many of our major projects at the studios.

Thank you to Celeste Cromack, an esteemed staff member of Nancy Renfro Studios, for serving as assistant editor in helping me to organize such complex material. Barbara Lindig also aided me in many ways towards the completion of material, and Debbie Sullivan, Joanne Click, Tamara Hunt and Connie and Jack Champlin, authors from previous collaborations, have all left their creative influence on this book.

Nancy Renfro

TABLE OF CONTENTS

Editor's Note:

Every child, male or female, has an enormous potential which begs to be realized. Therefore, in an effort to make the text, as well as the content, completely non-sexist, the dominant gender is switched from masculine to feminine, so as to avoid reading what "he" does on every page.

It did not seem quite right, however, to feminize all the personal pronouns, thereby committing the same injustice to men as has been committed to women by the exclusive use of the single-gender pronoun, whether that pronoun be "he" or "she." Therefore, until a good neutral term is developed in English to replace the cumbersome "he/she" combination, I have chosen to use the rather inconsistent but certainly well-intentioned method of switching genders throughout the text in order to achieve a note of balance. The reader's tolerance, and/or suggestions, are hereby requested.

Ann Weiss Schwalb
Chief Editor

INTRODUCTION
By Nancy Renfro

Puppetry, which represents the integration of sculpture, design, movement, expression and other elements of the arts has almost unlimited potential as a teaching and therapeutic tool—*Magic Fairy Hosiery and Box Puppet*

A Personal Perspective

By Nancy Renfro

I have been partially deaf all of my life. Cut off from the seemingly effortless communication that is so much a part of everyday life, I have been unwilling to consider myself handicapped. My personal survival hinged on a deep commitment to creative endeavors, especially in the realm of the visual arts. I was eager to try out all the media and like a sponge have, throughout my life, absorbed one applied art form after another—crayons, paint, paper, clay, and wood; and later, with career orientation in mind—graphics, architectural design and puppetry.

My handicap, classified as a nerve deafness, manifested itself at birth and resulted in a 40 percent hearing impairment that was especially acute in high frequencies. My big problem in childhood was the hearing aid which was a cumbersome affair. A network of wire linked a set of bulky batteries worn in a separate pouch with the receiver and large ear piece. The feeling and appearance were somewhat like being hooked up to a short wave radio! Although this early aid was helpful to some degree, it had the disadvantage of picking up extraneous noises and static. Since I was never forced to wear a hearing aid, I chose not to wear one on the grounds that I would be freer to explore my love for outdoor sports and games. Later, when I did choose to wear an aid, the stigma of being attached to such a device, which so vividly pointed out a deficiency, never bothered me as it did others. In fact, I generally welcomed people knowing I wore a hearing aid so they would make special effort to speak more clearly. But the stigma of being different, of being deficient in some physical sense, still remains for many of the disabled who must deal with various braces, wheelchairs and other such aids. As more positive attitudes emerge, I hope that someday all of these devices will be looked upon as both constructive and interesting, like the braces in orthodontistry. Certainly, aids are fascinating subjects of study for young children who often, with innocent curiosity, point to my ear and want to know, "What is that thing in your ear?"

My handicap, like all handicaps, presented me with a series of interesting problems. One had to choose between solving and conquering these problems or quietly slipping back. Until the recent widespread movement to raise consciousness and better the lives of our special persons population, slipping back was much more the norm. I believe that the principal reason for such behavior was that few educators knew effective ways to teach the handicapped. To relate to one who was different from the norm required a creative form of thinking as well as an in-depth understanding of the difference. I was fortunate the limitations bounding my handicap opened up an unusual pathway. Through the arts, I discovered a new language, one that is not classified as such but one which provided me with rich opportunity to grow.

There are three major areas with which a person with a disability such as mine must deal throughout life—*language, isolation*, and the struggle to maintain a *positive self-image*. Language is often one of the most challenging problems the handicapped child must confront. The hearing impaired, mentally retarded, multi-handicapped and sometimes those with emotional and learning disabilities must discover special ways to communicate with and relate to their outer worlds. Even the visually impaired person, who hears normally, has language barriers. This is especially true in the realm of descriptive language, for it is not easy to discuss or describe something one cannot see in terms similar to those used by one who is sighted.

Speech for me was slow in development and, as a result, few people understood me clearly. Until I was in third grade, my mother was the only person who was in tune with my distorted speech patterns in which *S* and *R* were outstandingly omitted. (The letter *S*, due to the fact that I could not hear the high pitch, and *R* because it was just too tricky.) It was interesting that a second grade teacher should point out my speech shortcomings, discovered while trying to teach the class Spanish! My mother was grateful that our school system was progressive enough to bring in a visiting speech therapist. To this day I remember the lessons clearly. The weekly sessions lasting nearly eight years, were the most boring class of my week. These early lessons were a repetitive diet of drills that never varied in format or approach and they were totally uninspiring from a young child's point of view. How I wished that this well-meaning speech teacher had had a puppet on hand!

Much of my speech improvement actually came from my parents' patience and their constant day to day corrections. But not until adulthood when I became a professional performer and lecturer in puppetry did I have motive and the dogged desire to pursue those long vanished *S*'s and *R*'s. I began again to take speech lessons. Thus I am an actual case study of the puppet's effectiveness as a tool in helping refine speech and develop public speaking skills.

In the meantime, while the verbal world played a minor part in my elementary years and early development, the visual world played a large and sustaining role. My mother can verify this fact as she describes the jammed drawerfuls of artwork she saved while I continued to dabble in various media. It did not occur to either of us that this pastime eventually would emerge into a special language of its own, one that illustrated feelings and ideas, as well as emotional and physical bonds to people and environment. However, the artwork remained in the drawers and, except for family, my communication outside the home still remained limited.

As far as my progress in school, education in those days was centered around a system that was purely verbal. Most teachers made a special effort to give me the best advantage in their classroom by giving me a good strategic location and repeating things when necessary. Despite considerate attempts by individual teachers to include me, most of the eight years in elementary level were passive ones spent daydreaming, window staring or clock watching. It was simply too much of a strain for this hearing impaired person to try to hear for long periods of time. The immediate result was poor academic grades. Fortunately, my behavior was excellent, but I can readily empathize today with behavioral problems that are often associated with a disability. It takes incredible discipline and patience to sit for five or six successive periods in a totally *passive* capacity.

Not until high school did others begin to understand my special language. Sewanhaka High School in Floral Park, New York was a marvelously stimulating school with 4,000 students and hundreds of vocational classes from which to choose. The instructors in art, sewing and cooking were superior; they were also ingenious at guiding and giving encouragement to students who exhibited talent in any given area.

I signed up for as many vocational classes as elective policy allowed. For the first time, I felt as if I really belonged; I had succeeded in finding other people who could relate to my artistic language. A mountain of growth occurred within me. Communication began and my shell of isolation was penetrated.

It is evident that the limitations set by a particular disability, no matter how minor, eventually establish a degree of isolation. In the case of a physical disability, such as a child with use of only one arm, this isolation might mean restrictions in physical activities, in the ability to build things and the like. But for a child with more profound handicaps, the limitations can be far reaching. The blind and physically disabled experience restricted mobility and often live in a world margined with narrow perimeters; the deaf child, who lacks total speech, has difficulty in socializing and interacting in general with the outside world.

As a hearing impaired child, isolation in various aspects of socialization has always been an element of my disability. A "friend" was defined in terms of someone who had incredible patience in repeating language to me, and also had insight into my handicap. I had only one friend throughout my elementary and high school years and most of our interaction was physical—sports and play. Socially, I was a wall flower and parties were a terror to me. They still are because it is impossible to hear above the drone of simultaneous conversations going on around me. Not until I began to relate to others in smaller select groups during college and my professional career, did socialization begin to flourish on its own.

Along with language and isolation, lack of self-esteem is the third common problem that the disabled person must conquer. Living a life of constant rejections by some must be balanced with a constant show of acceptance by others. The buoy in a handicapped child's life, it seems to me, is praise and encouragement. I have seen children at the Texas School for the Deaf in Austin perform for the first time on stage with Bodi-Puppets. After the performance, when applauded and told how wonderful they were, their eyes lit up and they visibly expanded with a new found sense of pride and, at least for the moment, with something akin to ecstasy. The children were so excited with the idea of performing for others and so long deprived of these experiences, that many of the children from the audience afterward came up to the dramatic teachers, tugged at their skirts, and asked if they, too, might have a chance to be on stage tomorrow! Few had any inhibitions at all about performing. The highlight of the show came when one child, who rarely used speech, suprised everyone by speaking her line as clearly and loudly as she could.

The nonhandicapped child knows what encouragement is all about. For this child, it is often a daily event and can be easily taken for granted. For the handicapped child, however, it is not readily available. If a child is deformed or appears unintelligent, we tend to repel the idea of touching, encouraging and praising, not realizing that this child, more than any other, needs an abundance of

reinforcement and encouragement. It is not possible for everyone to be an Anne Sullivan to a Helen Keller, but it *is* possible for those who work or in any way come into contact with a disabled child to be aware of the values and importance of positive reinforcements. Puppetry can help the adult in fulfilling this role. The mere act of letting disabled children perform in informal settings with puppets will involve children in public speaking and socialization practice, both of which may be a base for encouragement and building self-esteem.

In adulthood I take pride in having full command of my **alternate** language. Art has become a refined tool for me, a sharpening of my other senses, especially visual perception. Not only has art provided me a livelihood but it also has given me the unique ability to see the world as an artist sees it, a world that is an exciting montage of keenly animated visual pictures. Two people talking at the other end of a room, for example "speak" to me in terms of their shapes, the composition of the whole picture, their animation and coloration. Such mundane scenes are entirely aesthetic to me and from which I elicit much joy, scenes which I want others to experience so that they also can be enriched through alternate language. It is my fervent hope that the effort put forth in this book will help to expand the lives of others as art and the realm of puppetry have succeeded in enriching mine.

Why Puppets?

The value of the arts in teaching and bringing enrichment into the lives of the disabled is slowly gaining recognition throughout the country. More and more focal organizations such as the National Committee-Arts for the Handicapped, and the Kennedy Foundation espouse a philosophy that is far reaching and encompasses all of the arts, including puppetry. It is hoped that this firm support will continue to flourish and influence the overall quality of education for the disabled.

Puppetry, which represents the integration of sculpture, design, movement, expression and other elements of the arts has almost unlimited potential as a teaching and therapeutic tool. It remains, however, vastly underutilized in working with the disabled. The puppet's ability to adapt to the needs of the individual, taking into account both limitations and strengths, is an invaluable aspect of puppetry.

Since progressive methods for educating the disabled are relatively new, so too is the incorporation of puppetry into regular educational programming. To the teacher who is beginning to include puppetry in her work, thinking creatively and experimenting with unconventional approaches is an important and challenging aspect of working with disabled children. The teacher of the disabled student quickly learns that specific disabilities call for specific methods of application. This book attempts to present bold and innovative ways in which puppetry can be used as a tool to discover alternate routes to language. The power of the puppet lies in its strong, tangible, visual form which exists on an animated plane. By integrating visual and verbal aspects of this art form, language takes on a new dimension, providing reinforcement and motivation to the handicapped child. Puppetry can assist the teacher in achieving important educational objectives in skill development while expanding the disabled child's creative scope in several important ways.

• Developing Language and Communication Skills

Puppetry as a tool in the development of language and communication skills is the major focus of this study. A disabled child, who has been the object of much intense scrutiny both at school and at home, and whose differences are constantly pointed out, often experiences a sense of self-consciousness that can hinder the ability to communicate normally. A puppet can enable such a child to feel at ease, as it helps to redirect the focus away from the child. Serving as a facade behind which the child may temporarily take refuge, the puppet helps to pierce inhibitions and walls of shyness, as the child, using the puppet, focuses on what the puppet is doing or saying, rather than on the immobilizing fear of his own involvement in the process. The child believes in the puppet, in what it says and does, even though the child knows that he is, in fact, controlling what the puppet communicates. But so strong is the sense of communication with the puppet that an error committed by the puppet is attributed to the puppet rather than to the child, who is merely its conveyor. In this way, it is much easier psychologically, and much safer for the child to express certain ideas and feelings. As the puppet begins "to communicate" and take on a preeminent position, the child, in losing selfness, is finally able to unleash feelings and discover a sense of freedom in which expression and formulation of language can be manifested.

The approach taken in integrating puppets into a program to improve communication skills may be quite informal, as in using the puppet to converse with the child, simply to open up discussion and generate language practice. For example, an extremely shy hen puppet, who might have a similar visual impairment to the child, shares its frustrations in trying to find its way around the barnyard. Or, the activity may take on a slightly more direct course with improvised exercises to meet specific objectives. Perhaps the hen has trouble differentiating its *ch* and *sh* sounds. Together, child and hen can explore the words that begin with these sounds around the classroom or make-believe barnyard.

Specially designed puppets may be utilized for teaching language. Nancy Renfro Studios, for example, produces a Speech Pillow in which a large tongue, teeth and tonsils figure prominently for speech patterning. Or, a child-made Paper-Plate Puppet can be fashioned from two paper plates as described on page 70 and feature a large distinctive mouth and flexible tongue that can be used to illustrate speech sounds. A snake character makes the perfect vehicle for exploring the letter, *S*, or an owl the letter *O*. Bodi-Puppets, as described on page 59, are marvelously expressive tools for teaching deaf

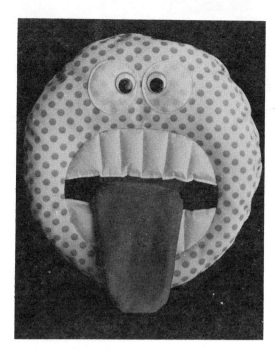

Speech Pillow by Nancy Renfro Studios

children sign language. Tactile puppets, which are comprised of a variety of textures, can open up avenues of exploration for blind children.

If a more structured approach is desired in expanding language skills, children may combine puppets with literature and have the opportunity to explore language in a broad sense. Through role playing, the children can be placed in active roles rather than passive ones, allowing them to become directly involved on a multi-dimensional level as stories are dramatized. New elements are added as movement through space, audio, visual and tactile aspects are incorporated into the story. If the child does not grasp the story's meanings because of an impairment of one or more of the senses, there is a good chance that some significant material will be assimilated through the strong sensory perceptions of the dramatization. Furthermore, some degree of learning is almost always assured as the combined sensory elements reinforce one another for a total learning experience. For example, a child playing the role of the Big Billy Goat in "Three Billy Goats Gruff" cannot escape the contrast between her own large lumbering movements and loud booming sounds, and those of the student next to her who portrays the Small Billy Goat. Thus, the child fully experiences the ramifications of big-little in several dimensions— visual, auditory and spatial.

Other elements of language conceptualization can be strengthened through children's active participation in such puppet stories. Spatial relationship (here and there) or frameworks of time (yesterday, today and tomorrow) are particularly difficult for deaf children to assimilate. In exploring literature with deaf students, intangible concepts can be better understood by encouraging children to dramatize these ideas within the context of the story. Characters can vividly illustrate the passage of space and time by their movement through physical space or even by scenery changes to mark time span, distance and location. These concepts, normally explained verbally, can be effectively portrayed with tangible forms, such as puppets and set designs.

Sequencing, that is, the capacity to order things or events, is an area of language development with which all children must struggle, to some degree. It is a particular stumbling block for hearing impaired students and those who suffer from a learning or emotional disability. But through the process of puppet dramatization with stories, the sequencing process is broken down into its component elements. Children, when using puppets, gain first-hand experience of the story's ordering as they divide the story into segments. Even making reference to scene changes or story setting helps to define and delineate sequence. A house, for example, can mark the beginning of "Little Red Riding Hood," a tree, the forest and ensuing middle sequence, and finally, grandmother's house can represent the closing segment of the tale. Children find these visual associations a great aid in remembering aspects of the story which otherwise might get jumbled together in their recollection. Also, because children are motivated by puppets in a way that is markedly different from an adult, they do not mind repeating a story for additional reinforcement, especially if interest is sustained by switching roles. After such an exercise, children can often recall the sequencing of the story even without the use of puppets, just because their concentration was so focused while puppets were being used.

The utilization of puppets for teaching language arts and discovering alternate routes to effective languages is virtually limitless. It is hoped that the individual teacher will not only be perceptive but daring as well in taking liberties to experiment with the ideas suggested in this book. Of primary importance is discerning what works well for the individual child and what does not. Searching for innovative solutions and continually seeking out new combinations of good ideas is essential for achieving the goals outlined.

• Overcoming Emotional and Physical Isolation

Isolation, which is a common problem among the disabled, is naturally countermanded with puppets, since puppets require a degree of interaction among the participants. The interaction may be simply that which exists between puppet and child. Or, it may be a triangle rapport between child, teacher and pup-

Communicative powers expand with the use of puppets

pet, or it may occur on a wider group level. As the child's communicative powers expand with the use of puppets as an intermediary, so too does the process of socialization, breaking down both emotional and physical isolation.

An easy way to begin overcoming the isolation of the disabled child is through the use of music with puppets. Songs and dancing are infectious in their involvement level and children, even deaf children, love music and rhythmical movements. Rhythm, whether it stems from the voice or the body, has primitive origins which bind individuals together in some sort of community. The communal sharing of rhythm has not only social value, but also therapeutic value. Rhythm is, in itself, a language that can communicate many things and is the premise upon which the section on "Kinetic Movement and Puppets" is based. In a sense, it is a silent language; even when words are present, the rhythm predominates and speaks first, imparting special

meanings to the child. Because many handicapped children experience only minimal group interaction, the leader will observe tangible results when applying these principles using puppets for group socialization activities.

In addition to rhythm, use of puppets can enhance group interaction through story dramatizations, general conversation, curriculum related games and related physical exercises, which all require a degree of interaction and response. The puppet alone, even without group involvement, can help in penetrating isolation. The puppet is a "friend" to the child and can be thought of in that way. A child who has difficulty communicating might find it less burdensome to speak privately with the puppet in expressing thoughts not otherwise revealed to an adult. Furthermore, the leader may use the puppet as a sort of go-between in communicating directly with the child.

The special child may experience a totally restricted kind of physical isolation due to lack of exposure to the environment. Frequently isolated from the physical world, the child who is disabled, especially one who is retarded, immobile or blind, may live an entire life span within the perimeters of a small and limited environment. For the severely retarded, this environment might be an institution, or even a single room; for others, it might be a single street or a school. When the child cannot physically cross boundaries to the rest of the environment, puppets can help bridge the gap between this restricted life style and the expanded world outside. Table-top Play, as described on page 57, makes excellent settings for exploring diverse environments—a productive farm, a colorful circus, a bustling city. The child can play with these settings, using Walking Finger Puppets, to span areas to which he might not otherwise have access or means to discover. The entire setting can be used as a base for studying that particular environment through miniature dramatizations or study unit activities. A productive farm, for example, gives opportunity for learning about farm animals, the types of enclosures they live in, daily farm life, how produce is grown and a host of other details.

Bringing the outside world within reach of the immobile child can also be done by introducing replicas of wildlife in an authentic environment. Realistic puppets such as an opossum or tiger can be used so that the child can touch it and more vividly visualize its appearance, its natural habitat and individual charactersitics.

Another form of physical isolation may be experienced by the disabled child who may lack personal contact. The need for physical contact, i.e., hugging, touching, caressing is an important aspect of early childhood development. When physical contact is absent, the normal developmental process is interrupted; the results of this deprivation are well documented in other literature. Due to a variety of reasons, there are some children who may not have experienced the requisite amount of cuddling, touching or physical play and are thus being deprived of a crucial aspect of their growth potential. Physical contact with a puppet can greatly benefit this withdrawn child, for it is perfectly acceptable that a puppet touch or cuddle a child, while such contact may not always be easily received from another person. Puppets have the capacity to interact through their easy expression of hugging, touching or rubbing hands with a child.

Physical play can also be introduced by the puppet, especially important when a child has had limited opportunity to play with other children in sports or games. A child and puppet can play ball together or engage in a friendly wrestle. Because the puppet is on the hands of a knowing adult, this rough housing can be done to a degree that is safe for the child, keeping physical and emotional abilities in mind. If at first a child appears frightened or reticent to engage in body contact, allow the child to gradually make contact with the puppet to a point that is comfortable to the child. Let matters proceed slowly, until fears are alleviated and the child feels comfortable accepting the approach.

Whatever form of isolation a child may experience, it is encouraging to know that puppets can aid in fulfilling many of the child's varying needs. Isolation in any form is perhaps one of the most painful experiences for the disabled child or adult. Breaking down the barriers which separate individuals from one another is an integral and inseparable part of our being, affecting our sense of completeness in life. Puppets can bridge the gap between isolation and communication, and help surmount both emotional and physical barriers.

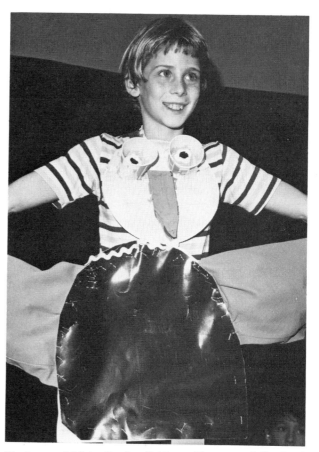

Placing a child in the limelight provides one of the best methods for raising self-esteem

• **Building Self-Esteem**

The mere act of performing or talking with the puppet is an activity that provides practice in public speaking skills for the child and helps in building self-confidence. The more opportunity the child has for communicating or dramatizing stories, activities and ideas through the puppet, the more facile will she become in communicating with people. Children who are able may wish to put on informal performances for their peers; such an experience places them in the limelight and provides one of the best methods for raising self-esteem. If a child is limited in the capacity to perform and can only achieve minor accomplishments, such as making the puppet say a few words or sentences, then be generous in praising this achievement. Genuine praise for acts which legitimately warrant praise and a steady diet of encouragement are the best ingredients to help motivate a child to try harder, speak louder, more clearly and generally feel better about her whole state of mind.

• Encouraging Emotional Release

Puppets and activities relating to puppetry offer a wide variety of socially acceptable outlets for release of emotions. Puppets can share the same emotion as the child and in releasing their feelings, offer a patterning process which the child may choose to follow. In addition, puppets can give the child an opportunity to see what would happen if emotions are released in a variety of ways. Furthermore, particular fears are unique to certain disabilities and in using the puppets, fears can be alleviated via the puppet. For example, the fear of bumping into things or falling is common to children who are visually disabled. In such a case, the instructor may use a puppet, perhaps a cat character, who is obsessed with the same fear and help the child to identify and deal with the fear. If the child uses the cat puppet himself, he may be able to explore hidden fears by instructing the cat to overcome the fears which he so vividly understands. By depersonalizing the situation and exploring the same fears in the context of the cat, the child is less threatened because, for the moment, they are not his fears. Moreover, being in the role of protector or instructor helps the child see that all the words explained to him by adults have some merit, as he now uses some of the very same explanations to alleviate the fears of the cat. There can't help but be some transference the next time the child experiences fear.

Puppets with aggressive characteristics, such as wolves or monsters, frequently appeal to children as a vehicle for venting their aggressive or angry emotions, often pent-up because they are less socially acceptable. Puppetry allows this healthy release to take place, and also provides a means to channel this aggression into constructive resolution or creative story development. Therapists working with disabled children may find puppetry an unusually effective tool in seeking out and exploring deep rooted problems. The use of role playing in the dramatization

of children's stories is perhaps one of the most constructive methods available for expressing a wide range of human emotions. Since stories and children's literature which display a broad range of emotional themes, i.e., fear, delight, sadness, insecurity are easily accessible, it is most interesting to try these techniques in exploring the spectrum of human emotions.

• Making Decisions

Generally, children with disabilities go through life with others often making decisions for them. The degree of their disability will impose limitations as to how much a child can decide for herself. The blind child has others choose the color clothing to wear, the mentally retarded has others decide what foods will be eaten and the physically disabled child must depend on others to determine what places she will visit. The experience of Tom Hudson, a sensitive librarian at the Pennhurst Center (State Hospital) in Spring City, Pennsylvania, illustrates how significant this lack of choice is. Tom, who uses puppets consistently with his residents, told of how much they enjoy visiting the library. Indeed, residents were strolling everywhere with books under their arms. With surprise, knowing that their reading level was quite low, a curious visitor asked Tom if they actually read all those books. "No," he replied, "but they enjoy more than anything *choosing* a book for

A rich assortment of diverse materials provides creative challenges for decision making

themselves." The library, it appears, is the only place in the entire institution where the residents can actually make a choice of their own, and the value that they placed on those books and the choice associated with it was heartwarming.

Puppetry offers decision making opportunities, especially in the construction of puppets themselves, in which there are choices to be made about what colors, materials or types of features a puppet should have. A rich assortment of diverse materials provides creative challenges for special children; in addition, such diversity will offer a meaningful experience in decision making. If a child is limited by a handicap and cannot cut, sew or perform such manual tasks easily, consider offering a selection of assorted pre-cut features to put onto the basic puppet. Even if only simple geometric shapes are offered, it is important that a selection is available. The features shown on page 74 may be reproduced for children to use in their puppet making endeavors. Advanced students will enjoy involvement in deciding details for integrated puppet presentations as well. Arranging props, creating background scenery, providing sound effects, or helping to block out the story's action all involve students in decision making puppetry activities.

- **Providing Physical Therapy**

Because puppets can be manipulated in so many ways, the physical therapist has an outstanding tool for specific exercises. A search through the wide range of puppet types will uncover a variety of puppets well suited for specific needs. Soft, comfortably fitting Hand Puppets with flexible bodies are excellent for developing small muscle dexterity in the hands; large Bodi-Puppets can be used for gross motor activities involving total body communications and Walking Finger Puppets for Table-Top Play can aid in hand/eye coordination. For those children who do not have sufficient motor control to operate puppets, consider such alternatives as simple Stand-Up Box Puppets or even the wearing of a Puppet Bracelet, which is an image tied to a ribbon on the wrist. Basic actions can center around these puppets by moving them along the tabletop or lifting the arm up and down to introduce exercise. All of these ideas are explored throughout the course of this book. Other puppets designed for specific purposes might take the form of a long knee sock snake character worn over the entire arm for slithering and encouraging arm exercises. Colorful shoes and fancy slippers can be converted into Foot Puppets (put eyes on them) for foot and leg muscles activities.

In summary, the puppet is an invaluable tool in working with disabled children. In the development of language, communication skills and socialization, its use is limited only by the degree to which the teacher's imagination can soar. Used in combination with other supporting art forms, it can give students significant experiences that can enhance their lives in a happy and meaningful way.

Understanding How the Special Child Sees

It is difficult, unless one has experienced the disability oneself, to understand just how a person with a handicap "sees." We too easily tend to gauge the world by our own personal sensory experiences and take for granted that everyone must receive information in a similar manner or express it in conformance. A perfect example is something as universal as color blindness. If everything the color blind person sees that is actually red appears to be orange, then how does this affect the total picture of his world? It has been proven that color has strong emotional impact on the individual, even going so far as to affect taste buds. The red stop light may take on a whole new meaning and the red apple a different taste, however, subtle, to the color blind person. If such a minor disability and differences as color blindness affects this person's world in profound ways, then how much more so is the world of a person with a larger disability affected? What are the various ways the Special Child sees?

- **The Hearing Impaired**

As a hearing impaired person, I am aware that I see the world in different tones and colorations from people with normal hearing. A simple example can be illustrated with the meeting of a new acquaintance. My initial reaction to a personality is based a great deal upon my response to that person's level of expression, rather than on specific speech or words chosen. I am often conscious of underlying subtleties that a particular gesture or facial expression connotes as the person speaks that perhaps are not detected by a hearing person, who concentrates more wholly on speech and specific words. As a result, my assessment of that person may differ totally from another's because I have been listening to the tune of a different language.

For the deaf, the eyes never stop seeing. If a child appears to miss out on a great deal of information because of a lack in hearing, the perceptive deaf child is indeed capable of compensating and finding other means for assimilating language and concepts. The child, who in skimming over the scene of a story, can pick out and remember minute details based on visual deductions has a marvelous tool at her disposal. The value of this unprocessed working material in the deaf child needs to be fully understood and channeled constructively if it is to be used as a potential basis for learning. Some educational theories adhere to the philosophy that the deaf child should conform fully to the nonhandicapped method of expressing language and completely discourage language through gesturing or signing. By insisting that a nonhearing child so fully conform to the hearing world, these theories discourage signing and the child's natural language is thwarted. The child's growth potential is limited by cutting off a central aspect of her ability to communicate.

• The Visually Impaired

Every person who works with a disabled population and wishes to more fully gain insight into how a visually impaired person sees should read *How Can I Make What I Cannot See* by Shiro Fukurai. Although this book deals solely with the subject of visual impairment, its sensitivity and soul searching ability to open up thinking can be applied to all areas. It is a small book and quickly read.

Fukurai, an art teacher in Japan, initially began work with many misconceptions about the blind. Through working with the media of clay, paint and drawing he eventually was able to more clearly understand the unique perceptual powers and limitations of blind children and their desire to create as others create. In the process, he also shaped a profound new philosophy for himself. The results, which were the children's works, were put on exhibit throughout Japan. The children with whom Mr. Fukurai worked had a sense of touch which was highly developed, but ironically they had never been taught to make things with their hands. At that time, even the children themselves had doubts about whether they could succeed. They too felt that if one cannot see, one cannot create.

In searching for materials, Fukurai ultimately reached the children through the medium of clay, and the results were powerfully revealing and touchingly sensitive. One of the first things he discovered was the truth in the parable of the three blind men and the elephant. The blind child often saw and emphasized those parts of the subject that were most prominent to that individual. For example, when asked to make a clay model of a house, without having seen a whole house before, a child created a flat plane of clay with an oversized doorknob on its surface. The doorknob represented the significant feature to the child and its size and positioning gave strong clues to his relationship to the house as a whole. Another example is the model of a dog. Since the blind child experiences "seeing" a dog by feeling it from one end of the body to the other, and then downwards, one leg at a time, the finished model is shaped much like a bear skin rug with all fours spread outwards.

The blind child's conception of space is also an interesting one which profoundly affects his interpretation of the world. While the sighted person's view of his environment is strongly defined by planes, shapes and forms—walls, fences, sidewalks, houses, vehicles, etc.—the blind person's picture is influenced by the spaces between and how he ambulates through these spaces. The walls serve predominantly as reference points and perimeter guidelines to these spaces, which are the key elements to a visually impaired person. Thus, when asked to create a model of a bus, Fukurai's child created a long hollow space in which the floor board was prominent, again because in the child's experience, a bus was an elongated opening with a floor to stand on.

It is also interesting to note the blind child's conceptualization of human beauty is a pleasing voice and smooth skin. Such abstract ideas are deeply internalized in shaping this child's viewpoint of the world. It is of primary importance, that we, as teachers, are finely tuned into the sensitivity of the disabled child and use it as a pivotal point from which to communicate. If we tell the child that a particular person is actually ugly, in spite of the person's soft voice and lovely skin, then we are depriving this child of an important message in an already limited perceptual mode. It is far more important to accept the child's concept of beauty and use it as a base for further development, searching out other things that can be described in similar terms. The teacher can benefit by using this same frame of reference to teach concepts. For example, exercises that expand upon smooth, textures and pleasant sounds can be explored as a means of expanding descriptive vocabulary in describing what is beautiful and what is ugly, and then moving on to other concepts.

It is apparent from the lessons of the blind that all persons, even those without a disability, see the world in symbols as well. A perfect illustration is to ask a nonhandicapped child to draw a house. The image is nearly always the same, a square with a triangular roof. Asking him to draw a car, a person or apple produces similarly predictable results. The conclusion we can surmise is that we so fully acclimate ourselves to seeing the world as a series of symbols that we often take for granted that others see the world using the same images. These symbols become a baseline for communication and language, one which the disabled child, who often sees the world in either "different" or distorted terms does not have, until taught.

Refreshingly, it is the young child, the artist and often times the disabled (particularly hearing and visually impaired) who can pare away the conformity of symbolism and see things in an original way, which reflects a sensory response that is pure and nonconditional.

In the artistic creations of Fukurai's children, symbolic imagery as well as strong emotional responses, were expressed. The clay models which the children built were indeed highly distorted, due to lack of sight, in their visual interpretation. However, they expressed a vitality of spirit that encompassed a full range of human emotions—love, anger, frustration and joy, to name but a few.

• **The Physically Disabled**

The physically impaired child, of all the handicapped, may be the least restricted in the way she sees. However, if a child has never experienced the simple feats of walking or running, then she may more aptly view the world in terms of one that does not include these activities or perhaps go to the opposite extreme, that of becoming obsessed with them. Also, the limitations of mobility may confine the child, as it does for the mentally retarded, to a microworld of one room (if bedridden), or a narrowed environment comprised of school, home or neighborhood. Consequently, reality-based themes are suggested in first reaching this child and gradually expanding horizons to wider vistas. Table-Top Play, as

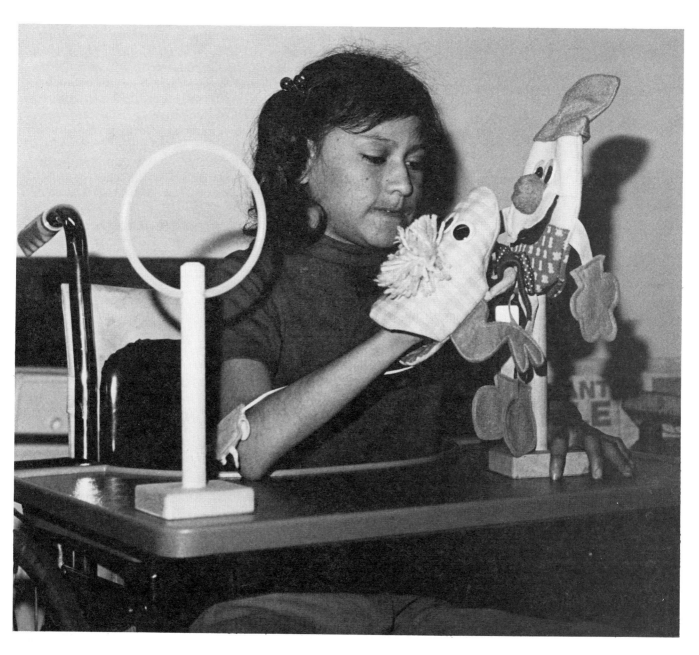

A physically disabled child participates in Table-Top Play

described on page 57, are excellent activities for both the mentally retarded and physically disabled in introducing them to other environments—the farm, city, zoo, etc.

• The Learning Disabled

The learning disabled child also sees in unique ways. It has only been recently discovered that this disability does not reflect upon intelligence, as evidenced by both Thomas Edison and Albert Einstein, who were known to have had learning disabilities. The learning disabled child does not perceive or express information in the same way as what is considered the norm. When the difficulty manifests itself in reading or writing or numerical skills, this child, when asked to conform to the norm, becomes frustrated because he cannot conform and begins to set up barriers. Although progress in learning might be slow, the results are well worth the effort. Here, too, one must sensitize oneself to the way the child sees and try to understand the commonplace events that are stumbling blocks to the child. Confusing similar letters such as *D* or *B*, reversing words or numerals, or orientating himself in space are typical problems for the learning disabled child. The activities described in the section on "Kinetic Movement and Puppets," are especially well-suited for children in coming to grips with the limitations accompanying their disabilities.

• The Mentally Retarded

The mentally retarded child often sees the world in distorted ways. The distortion might be a limited view of the world, narrowed down even further by the perimeters of a restricted physical environment and/or mental abilities. In some cases, the narrowed perimeters can be quite severe especially for those children who live in institutions and are capable of minimal growth potentials, either mentally or physically. The world that this child sees is a non-expanding one, one that centers around a strong reality base—food, sleep, family and staff members. Thus, it is important in educating or using puppets with this child, to use strong reality-based themes and gradually expand outwards from these points to tangential environments.

• The Emotionally Disturbed

The emotionally disturbed child's view of the world is also a distorted one, that is greatly influenced by whatever specific fears she retains, these fears often hindering growth. If the child has an emotional block due to a specific cause such as an inferiority complex because of a physical deformity or some less tangible reason, this negative feeling may restrict the child's ability to socialize normally. She may see the environment as a negative one, filled with hostile people and dangerous forces and begin to recede into a withdrawn state. This child may, in some ways, be more restricted than children with other handicaps for a severe emotional block can create a dead end for educational or emotional growth potential. Puppets, used properly, can aid the teacher greatly in making contact with these children and talking out and role playing their problems in a more effective way than traditional educational approaches.

Learning to see then, as others see, is of primary importance to the educator in whatever activity or medium is planned. For some, this perceptual ability comes easily; for others it is a matter of hard work, training and reorientation. Working with children who have a particular disability, tuning in to what they say and do and keying into their personal symbolism is one of the best methods of understanding and making contact. Together with this sharpening perceptivity, flexible thinking is crucial. It is important to rid oneself of stereotypic ideas of what is normal or "right". If beauty can be judged by the blind in terms of a soft voice and lovely skin, and by the deaf in terms of animated vibrancy when speaking, then let us call it so. For if the disabled have much to learn from us as teachers, we also have opportunity to learn from them in teaching us alternate ways to see.

Books About the Special Child

Books, Puppets and the Mentally Retarded Student. John and Connie Champlin. Special Literature Press, 1980. Omaha, NE.

A well structured book with excellent ideas to lead mentally retarded students into an appreciation of literature through puppetry. Includes a participator approach.

How Can I Make What I Cannot See? Shiro Fukarai. Van Nostrand Reinhold, 1969, New York.

A superb, easy-reading book that gives insight into the artistic accomplishment of blind students written by a sensitive art teacher in Japan.

Like It Is: Facts and Feelings About Handicaps From Kids Who Know. Barbara Adams. Walker and Co. 1979, New York.

An excellent book written by children for children to read to find new understandings on what a particular handicap is like. A very personal story.

The Music Came From Deep Inside. Junius Eddy. McGraw-Hill Co. 1982, New York.

A series of stories and essays of artists and severely handicapped children. A dancer, actress, musician, visual artist and puppeteer explore new ways of reaching, motivating and teaching these children.

Pocketful of Puppets: Activities for the Special Child With Mental, Physical and Multiple Handicaps. Debbie Sullivan—illus. by Nancy Renfro. Nancy Renfro Studios, 1982. 1117 W. 9th Street, Austin, TX 78703.

An excellent book to open up horizons for adults who work with the Special Child. Simple activities centered around table top theatres, bodi-puppets, puppet bracelets and others.

Puppets and Therapy. A.R. Philpott. Plays, Inc. 1977. Boston, MA.

A comprehensive book of many short essays explaining random projects with puppetry and the disabled.

What If You Couldn't. Charles Scribner's Sons, 1979. New York.

For young adult readers, it clearly illustrates and provokes thinking in areas of the handicapped. Examples are given such as what if you were missing an arm or leg, or what if you could not see?

DISCOVERING KINETIC LANGUAGE
By Cynthia Roup Harp

Cynthia Roup Harp has taught rhythm class at the Texas School for the deaf in Austin for six years. She is an innovative teacher in her work with exploring hidden potential in deaf students through body movement and creative dramatics. She presently resides in Austin with her husband, Steven, and two young children, Celina and Ariel Seth.

Nonverbal forms of communication can help to enliven the spirit and help the child blossom—*Hosiery and Box Bodi-Puppet*

Discovering Kinetic Language

By Cynthia Roup Harp

Kinetic language is the language of movement, a language in which dance, creative dramatics and rhythm all play a part. Although one might question the importance of creative movement in the special education curriculum, it is the disabled child who absolutely needs these very disciplines. Children with disabling conditions must spend greater amounts of time learning basic subjects in order to prepare themselves to be self-sufficient members of society. Their time in the classroom is precious and consequently, one may question the value of creative movement lessons. The approach and theories outlined in this chapter rest on the premise that the development of movement skills is really prerequisite to the development of intellectual skills and that interaction with the immediate environment enhances the learning of abstract concepts. Educators have known for some time that we have largely focused on training only the left hemispheric activities of the child: the reasoning, analytical and linguistic modes. Educators are now realizing the tremendous value of maturing the "whole child" by placing more emphasis on right hemispheric functions as well. Through the inclusion of creative arts activities—dramatics, music and art—such programming efforts can significantly increase the effectiveness of traditional teaching methods. For the special child whose method of thinking may be circumscribed by a particular disability, it is especially important that alternate channels of learning are introduced in order to complement the teaching of academic skills.

In the activities which follow, we are ultimately concerned with the development of language and its effect on social integration of the special child. Body movement is directly related to the art of social integration and is an inherent expressive form in all human beings. A baby learns to communicate successfully with parents through movement and gestures. As we go through life, consciously or subconsciously, we continue to use this body language for other types of communication. Sometimes, however, our verbal forms of communication become so overwhelmingly sophisticated that there is little use or little emphasis on nonverbal language forms. Such nonverbal forms as body language and rhythm projection, remain relatively unexplored and ineffectual. Certain perfunctory words in our western culture are universally communicated through gestures: yes, no, good-bye. A few other gestures survive such as shrugging shoulders for "I do not know," stamping a foot in anger, or hitting the forehead with a palm to indicate something forgotten. These gestures, however, remain only the tip of the vast resource of expressions that can be utilized for body articulation in expressing a silent language.

According to the principles of Paige and Hans Furth on child development, the sequence of learning begins with the child's interaction with the immediate environment. This initial direct contact and concrete experimentation with the physical world is necessary before the child can progress to abstract modes of understanding. A child initially gains knowledge of her own body, its strengths as well as its limitations. Then she proceeds to a knowledge of her surroundings, and finally begins to comprehend how she relates to her environment. All this development precedes the more difficult task of grasping and translating verbal languages. For example, before a child understands the permanency or reality of objects, she experiences the "peek-a-boo" game. Through this physical activity, she learns the concept that out of sight is *not* necessarily out of existence. This complex idea manifests itself through movement in the child's mind. Thus, restriction in the child's ability to move freely at an early age is, in essence, an intellectual restriction. Excessive use of playpens, for example, is a disservice to the child— even when objects in the playpen are changed frequently—because a major source of information, that of exploring the surroundings, is cut off. This major problem confronts the special child who experiences physical limitations due to a particular disability, whether physical, mental or emotional. So for the young child and older child alike, exploring and discovering the world and oneself through physical activity is a prerequisite for the successful development of the child's language.

The Movement Activities

Although the primary focus of this book is language and communication, it is difficult to discuss these elements in isolation for they serve as a foundation that links the individual with almost every aspect of life. The activities that follow show how a particular nonverbal form of language, creative movement, can be used as a base with which to enlarge the world of the special child.

All of the movement activities included herein are designed to help familiarize the disabled child with his body and build awareness in body rhythm and its unique language. Informal and loosely structured activities demonstrate various techniques of using the body in a conscious effort towards learning. The broad range of projects center around such activities as tension releasing techniques for relaxing parts of the body, mirroring games for allowing the child to follow directional movement, and color and sound response activities that teach specific concepts such as antonyms, numbers and shapes. The last group of activities concentrates on story development and imagination.

The leader will enjoy finding ways to vary and expand upon the individual movement activities. For example, if an activity is designed around the children's response to colored shapes, changing the shapes into numbers or even substituting words for the shapes will revamp the activity, thus creating a new lesson with new information to be imparted. Or, if an activity calls into play the use of the entire body, consider restructuring it to focus on isolated body parts, especially for a child with physical limitations. A child in a wheelchair, for example, who may only have movement in the upper portions of the body can use arms and head for mirroring games. The needs and limitations of exceptional children must always be taken into account when attempting movement activities and the sessions should be adapted accordingly. **Consultation with a therapist is recommended when there is any reason to question an individual's ability to handle a planned activity.**

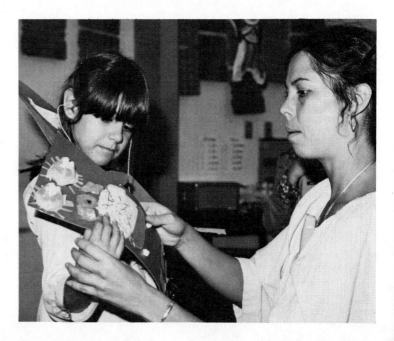

30

A child wearing a Shape Puppet is assisted by Cynthia Roup Harp—*Shape Activity*

Creative Movement and Expression Using Bodi-Puppets

The following discussion of six disabling conditions shows that all children are capable of creative movement. Creative movement activities, as described in this chapter, can be designed or modified to reinforce mental concepts, improve muscle control and reflexes, familiarize the child with physical capabilities, or permit expression of feeling.

Additionally, wearing a Bodi-Puppet permits a child to become the puppet character and put aside inhibitions and sense of embarrassment. Many children tend to avoid anything new. They are particularly evasive if an area of incapacity is involved. This two-pronged approach to creative movement—utilizing Bodi-puppets and gradually introducing activities—gives the comfort of being "someone else" and encourages successful, unselfconscious response.

• The Hearing Impaired Child

The vast majority of deaf children are unique in that their primary means of communication is through movement of their body parts. Whether their message is conveyed through sign language or gestures, the deaf are keenly aware of body language and how it communicates. Because it is so natural for them to express themselves with their bodies, it is important for us to acknowledge this perceptual talent and guide them into using body language to communicate more effectively. Studies show that language is the most difficult area of development for the deaf. The difficulty they encounter in structuring their thoughts into a linguistic system is compounded since they can often be communicated through movement or gestures. Deaf children with low verbal skills are able to express freely many of their inner thoughts through creative movement.

The hearing impaired child may not have the vocabulary or mastery of language structure to communicate such abstract emotions as pride in learning to ride a bike, or frustration in being excluded from play with hearing peers. But these emotions can be given release through movement activities and can even be communicated through nonverbal modes of communication. On the other hand, the hearing impaired child who is quite capable of expressing emotions, needs and thoughts through verbal communication, can learn greater creative expression in language through movement, dramatics and mime activities. The activities in this section will provide a basis for more creative thought processes and expression. Therefore, the nonverbal forms of communication can enliven the spirit and help the child blossom.

Hearing impaired children need not be excluded from the activities which entail response to music. Even the most profoundly deaf child will be able to respond to music, to some degree, particularly if it is a percussive sound (drum, piano, xylophone) and is played loudly enough. The vibrations created by these instruments will travel through the air and along the floor, especially wooden floors, and be felt by the child through the body. The hearing impaired child will be able to actually "feel" the sound, even though unable to hear it.

Bodi-Puppets make superb partners in learning activities with deaf students since signing can occur in front of the puppet's body or face. A child may need some time to get used to the idea of transferring sign language to the puppet's face rather than her own, but such signing can be easily achieved with practice. If transference of sign to the puppet's face appears to frustrate the child, permit the child to sign around her own face instead.

A handicapping condition appears to benefit from specific movement activities. Although the Bodi-Puppet is optional in pursuing the activities, its addition serves to further enrich the experience.

• The Visually Impaired Child

Because a blind child encounters great difficulty maneuvering freely within the environment throughout life, movements tend to be stilted, calculating and stiff. How important it is for such a child to be able to express more freedom of movement, to feel the joy of expressing emotions and to identify more closely with the body by building a stronger, positive self-image through movement activities.

The blind child is usually so unaccustomed to moving freely through space that the instructor must be careful to introduce such activities gradually, beginning, perhaps, with rudimentary exercises dealing mostly with body awareness and sensitivity. These introductory basics might include isolation of body parts such as freely moving an arm or a finger during an activity or in discovering how many ways the child can move his foot, then arms, before asking him to utilize the entire body in space. Limiting the space within which the child can move is important so that the child may better familiarize himself with the perimeters of the environment. Such well-defined space gives the child an additional sense of security in which to try the exercises suggested in this book.

Incorporation of sound and/or touch activities will serve as an excellent foundation for other learning experiences while appealing additionally to the intrinsic perceptual abilities of the visually impaired child. "Dance Tempo" or a touch version of "Poses" are excellent to explore. By engaging in these activities, a visually impaired child who has experienced the fear of movement in space will have opportunity to alleviate some of that fear.

Whole-body creative movement for blind children should take place in a restricted area that is cleared of obstacles. Boundaries should be marked by materials that will not injure the child if he collides with them. Large soft pillows or cardboard boxes make good barriers or a rope could be used, when suspended at waist height and attached to non-injurious supports. The instructor should guide the child on a tour of the activity space to familiarize him with the boundaries before suggesting whole-body creative movement.

Bodi-Puppets serve as bold and colorful visual forms on which children with some distinguishing sight can easily focus. Tactile puppets are particularly exciting to explore with these children. Yarn or cording, buttons and bottle caps, or thick cardboard cutouts can be glued to the face area to create features that can be felt with the fingers. Burlap, aluminum foil, cotton, yarn, sandpaper and other tactilely diverse materials should also be part of puppet making projects when working with blind or visually impaired students. An evil character may be created from rough, unpleasant feeling materials while soft, pleasing materials might suggest a beautiful character.

The puppet becomes an accessory to the blind child as he moves in space and learns such things as cane mobility, traffic safety, socialization skills and story dramatization, together with the movement activities described in this section.

• The Physically Impaired Child

The possibility of creative movement for the physically impaired child is a highly individual matter which will depend on the type of condition and degree of motor limitation. Because a child is restricted in a particular part of the body is no reason to restrict other areas as well. Although additional restriction is unfortunately common, it is a real disservice to the child; as a result the child's superior body parts become underdeveloped, together with the disabled body part. The child who is confined to a wheelchair or even to a bed still has many areas of the body that can function in creative expression activities. One needs only to choose those activities which isolate the feet, ankles, toes, arms, shoulders, fingers, hands, head, facial muscles and spine.

Physically impaired children are included in the activities in this section in hopes that they will enjoy participating within the framework of their individual movement potential. It is the teacher's role to help these children in adapting the activities to suit the needs and capabilities of the individuals, and to

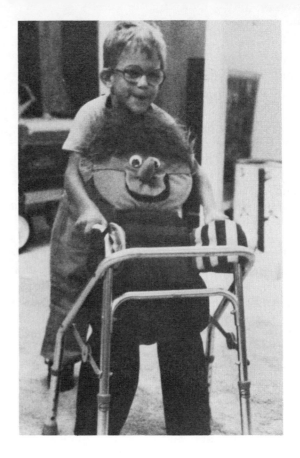

allow these children to participate alongside their peers, to the extent that they are able. The instructor needs to instill more joy of movement into the physically disabled child, remembering that this child has often missed out on some very basic movement processes. If a child is not able to join classmates in specific movement activities, a place can be found for other kinds of participation, including playing a musical instrument, calling out directions, or holding ropes, hoops or other props. Sometimes a slight bending of the rules is all that is necessary to include this child in the activity. Before proceeding with any of these activities, be cautious; consult a therapist if you are unsure about the child's physical abilities.

As an inducement to involve the physically impaired child in movement activities, the Bodi-Puppet can open new realms of discovery. A child in a wheelchair or on crutches will find as much pleasure in wearing these puppets as any other child. If a child is missing an arm or other body part, consider making puppets with a corresponding disability. Letting the child know that puppets also must work around a particular disability can ease the sense of isolation and help the child accept his or her own limitation with more understanding.

• The Learning Disabled Child

The learning disabled child often has difficulty with spatial relationships, which is most commonly evidenced in difficulties this child exhibits in reading or writing activities. Much work can be done on building basic awareness of spatial orientation skills through creative movement. When the child is able to orient herself successfully in larger spatial relationship experiences through body movements, then a transference can be more easily made to the finer spatial relationships required in writing and reading.

A learning disabled child who has difficulty with writing letters properly may benefit from such activities in this chapter that involve moving the body along certain patterns such as the "Abstract Shape" or the "Body Letter" activities, and may enable the child to understand the concept of directionality and therefore be able to comprehend shapes and letters and to reproduce them.

The "Mirroring" activity (leader stands facing the student, who copies movements like a mirror image) can sometimes be very difficult for the learning disabled child. If so, the teacher should stand beside the child or have the child stand behind the teacher in order to better copy a movement.

Many of the movement activities in this section are designed purposefully to take the body through space. By working with these concepts, the learning disabled child can gain some degree of mastery over an orientation that previously caused problems.

The Bodi-Puppet offers excellent opportunities for hand/eye coordination activities, as well as exploring larger movements with the learning disabled child. Here, as in other cases, the puppet takes the focus away from the child in providing a nonthreatening environment and any errors or shortcomings by the child can be quickly transferred to the puppet.

• The Mentally Retarded Child

Learning is often a slow process for the mentally retarded child and creative movement can aid this child in many areas, particularly in understanding abstract concepts and in improving motor coordination. The retarded child, struggling with difficult-to-grasp concepts, will find certain things better understood through participatory movement activities in which the child experiences a direct relationship to the concept being presented. For example, the child can be told that the book is on the *high* shelf or the *low* shelf. At first he may appear confused but through the kinetic actions of actually reaching up high or stooping down low the concept is better understood. Other spatial concepts such as *over, under* and *around*; emotions such as *happy, sad* and *angry*; simple math concepts; and language concepts such as adjectives and prepositions can all be reinforced in a similar manner. The leader may wish to design individualized activities based on some of those included in this chapter to meet specific objectives toward concept learning.

It is important for the brain-damaged child to improve his sensory motor skills because often his coordination is poor. In so doing, the child can begin to identify better with his body, developing positive self-images and using it as a frame of reference from which to make perceptions. The retarded child frequently participates only minimally in the physical activity and games which are a natural part of childhood. Thus, adults working with this child need to make a conscientious effort to select activities which develop and refine hand-eye coordination and general body balance. Many of the exercises in this section are helpful in meeting these objectives. The response activities such as the "Fast to Slow" are excellent for learnng body coordination control, while the "Knees and Toes" activity serves to focus on slightly finer motor skills. It is best to begin slowly in introducing an activity to the brain-damaged child; it is also extremely important to know his limitations and not to frustrate these limitations. If the child feels he is performing the simple exercises well, he will be more apt to want to try more advanced ones later. Remember that this child may also have weakened and unused muscles which may take repeated sessions over a period of time to strengthen. Repetition of the activities, with variations when possible, is a key to helping this child grow.

The Bodi-Puppet is a strong visual focus to help motivate the mentally retarded child to participate in numerous experiences. If this child feels reluctant to perform because he learns slowly, this feeling is quickly transferred to the puppet rather than the child. The mentally retarded child particularly enjoys role playing through these puppets and in doing so will be given opportunity to try on life situations in new and nonthreatening ways, perhaps not otherwise possible.

• The Emotionally Disturbed Child

Inner emotions are often difficult for people to express verbally. This is particularly true for the child who is emotionally disturbed. The magnitude of this child's emotions is so vast and exaggerated that understanding, expressing and controlling these emotions becomes a grave challenge and this child's failures can interfere with many facets of life.

Emotional conflicts can be improved by the physical expression through movement activities shown in this section. These activities are ideal for the child who needs help in coming to terms with and learning to cope with internal strife and emotions. The emotionally disturbed child can learn how to control these emotions through the direction and mastery of body movements. Learning to control the body as well as give it a sense of order makes it easier to bring emotions into line.

It is advisable that any creative movement activity in which an emotionally disturbed child might be involved be discussed with the child's therapist, both for reasons of safety as well as extra insight that may be provided. The therapist may be able to suggest specific movement activities that would benefit the child and will advise the instructor also if an activity is unsuitable.

Kinetic energy may be a channeled and restrained emotion that can be safely released through the vehicle of the Bodi-Puppet. Role playing greatly benefits the emotionally disturbed child because it provides opportunities to learn to cope with deeply rooted feelings by "trying on" life situations using the puppets. Such situations, in a controlled and nonthreatening environment, provide the child with immensely rewarding and productive opportunities to learn.

Planning the Activities

The instructor planning to use the creative movement activities suggested in this chapter need not have had prior experience in any form of dance, dramatics or music. As a whole, the activities require minimal skills. It is perhaps more important for the instructor to be open-minded in trying out ideas which may serve as guidelines for adding future projects or in creating variations of existing movement activities. If the teacher feels that it is not feasible to designate time for a project, take short "movement breaks" from the regular classroom routine. Engage the children in five minute activities which will refresh them and can build eventually into an effective learning experience.

It is not necessary to have a large space to perform the movement activities. If the classroom is all that is available, push the desks aside or, for brief movement exercises, let the children perform in a standing or sitting position on the floor next to their desks. A number of the exercises can actually be conducted at the desks, if movements are isolated to the upper part of the body. Ideally, of course, it would be convenient to find a larger space away from the classroom routine which the group can use on a regular basis.

Use of small mats or carpet samples make floor activities special for the children. Many like to have their own particular square and choose a certain color or pattern each time while others prefer to choose a different one each time. Gym mats may be laid on the floor to enable the severely disabled to participate in exercises from a reclining position.

When planning space for blind students, consider delineating certain areas for reasons of safety with rope barriers, a low wall of pillows, mattresses, gym mats or other solution. These students will enjoy being allowed to move freely without restraint in a given space. Varying the shape of the space can lend interest in programming projects for the blind. For example, the perimeters of the space may be linear, circular or square at successive periods. Blind students will also delight in choosing their own sound makers and selecting their own musical ensembles with which to improvise sounds. Be sure to have a particularly rich assortment of musical and toy instruments, as well as found objects for exploring tactile sounds.

There is no rigid pattern for planning the movement activities in this chapter. Selecting activities at random to suit mood or need is perfectly acceptable. The novice instructor of movement might wish to begin with the simpler projects such as "Fast to Slow" or "Mirror Game" and eventually work up to more advanced ideas. It is helpful for the leader to inform the children at an early stage the predesignated signal for stopping when "freeze" is required in activities. "Freeze" is that moment when all motion is stopped, within an exercise, and the children temporaily remain stationary. A follow-up signal is then issued to cue the children to proceed with movement again. The signal may be a specific sound from an instrument, clap of hand, upraised arm or other distinctive sign.

If time permits and certain physical or educational objectives are sought, then the instructor may wish to formulate a more structured program, perhaps following the general suggested sequencing of activities in this chapter. Or, a specific focus may be intended and all activities can evolve around reinforcing this focus such as exploring self-concepts, vocabulary or sensory skills. Correlated classroom activities may also link or follow-up on strengthening the individual focus. For example, after a movement activity on building self-concepts, the children could be asked to write or draw positive things about themselves in a language arts or drawing project. Interrelating movement activities to other aspects of the curriculum will bring more significance to each exercise while reinforcing the concept at varying levels. After a vigorous movement activity, it is best to end these sessions with a calming activity such as the "Reach for a Star activity," or simply have the children lie down and feel their breath as they inhale and exhale, breathing deeply, or to simply lie quietly with eyes closed and soft music playing. This helps settle the children down for their next planned activity session.

Using Sound with the Activities

Musical instruments provide a valuable dimension and enrichment to the sessions in adding sensory stimulation. Commercially made rhythm instruments such as drums, xylophones, cymbals, wood blocks are fun to include in activities. Other types of noisemaking equipment may be substituted if these instruments are not readily available. Capitalize upon tonal differences between cooking pots, cardboard boxes and wooden blocks. The sound of styrofoam blocks clapping together can be effectively alternated with the different sound of a lid being banged with a spoon or you can devise an exercise that experiments with different percussive sounds. Children will probably offer their own inventive suggestions about rhythmic noisemaking. To store sound makers, decorate cardboard cartons with gayly colored gift wrap or shelf paper and write in bold letters on the front "Sound Makers." Here are some items to include in your Sound Making Bins.

Homemade Instruments

—Pots and pot lids
—Baking pans of varying sizes
—Metal and wooden spoons of varying sizes
—Styrofoam packaging blocks, as found in
  appliance packages
—Wood blocks
—Wood dowels
—Cardboard tubes of varying sizes
—Sturdy food and staple boxes (salt, oatmeal,
  detergent, egg cartons, etc.)
—Metal pails
—Paper paint buckets
—Wash board
—Cheese grater
—Grocery cartons

Commercial Instruments

—Sand Blocks
—Castanets
—Rhythm sticks
—Guiro
—Xylophone
—Drum
—Cymbals
—Maraca

The Bodi-Puppets

The introduction of Bodi-Puppets with these activities provides exciting visual focus in redirecting attention away from the child toward the puppet while an action is being performed. If time does not permit, then the activities of course may be conducted without Bodi-Puppets. However, Bodi-Puppets, as described on page **XX**, are simple to make and can be imaginatively constructed from large grocery bags and scrap materials. These puppets are ideally suited to partner movement as they are worn in front of the child's body and become a natural extension to the child's movements. A repertory cast can be made at the outset of the sessions and reused multiple times. Young children enjoy making a variety of animals such as barnyard or jungle creatures, while older children prefer monsters, science fiction characters or a basic people cast. The flat grocery bags can easily be stored away or hung on a clothesline or wall for display when not in use.

Body pictures are also excellent for using with movement activities. They are easily constructed and can be changed quickly to complement each activity. These impromptu costumes, whether a drawing, magazine page, poster or photograph, are merely suggestive to the child as they are attached to the front of the body in the chest area. Pictures of a fox, snake, farmer, chef, baby, king, or other image are appropriate in creating identities while movement is explored. These pictures may include vehicles (a spaceship or train), nature elements (water, sun and flower), inanimate objects (a broom or teapot) and abstract concepts images (digits and shapes). Animate and inanimate imagery are exciting when used in conjunction with movement exercises because they help children form a visual picture of the concept they are portraying.

Sun

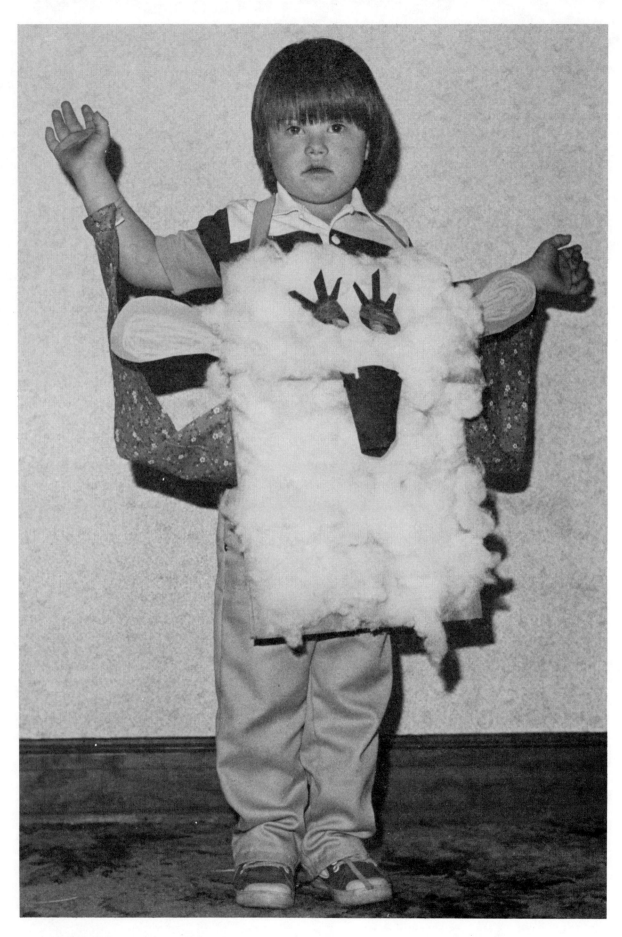

It is important for the disabled child to be keenly tuned into his body's abilities—*Sheep Bag Bodi-Puppet*

Body Awareness and Sensitivity Activities

It is important for the disabled child to be keenly tuned into his body's abilities, to cultivate an awareness and sensitivity of it. These activities are designed to draw the child's attention to his body, to give him increased consciousness of the various body parts and to instill in him an extra amount of sensitivity of the body's rhythms and how it can relate to group rhythms as well. These activities will aid the child by giving him opportunities to know his instruments of expression more fully. It is through these areas that the child is building a foundation for the future development of more positive self-image, and eventually more sophisticated social and linguistic skills.

• Fast to Slow

The purpose of this exercise is to take the children through a very fast, vigorous activity and then a very slow, quiet activity. This contrast allows them to experience different energy levels. Build a signal into the activity to indicate when the action changes such as a clap of hands or drum beat.

Have the children:

— *run around the room quickly and shout (one at a time to avoid confusion and too much noise), then crawl very slowly on the floor as if extremely heavy.*

— *shake their bodies all over as fast as possible; then walk as if a lighted candle is on top of the head. They should move very carefully so that the candle will not fall off or blow out.*

— *move as if electricity is going through their bodies; then tell them someone has turned off the electricity. (The leader can pretend to turn off a "switch" on each child's arm or back.)*

— *walk around the room, flinging out arms, stamping feet, shaking heads; then lie down on the floor and breathe deeply for three long breaths with eyes closed and imagine they are very light, floating on top of a big, white, billowy, cloud in the clear, blue sky while the wind blows gently over their bodies.*

• Fast to Slow with Props

This is an expansion of the previous activity with the addition of props to give interest. Have a collection of everyday items on hand but avoid using anything sharp, pointed, or awkward to carry. A book, broom, ball, pencil, rope, mixing spoon and bowl are fun to include.

Discuss the concepts of *fast* and *slow* with the children. Ask for examples of tasks that are done fast and tasks that are done slowly. Suggest things that happen fast (explosion of a firecracker) and things that take a long time (bread dough rising).

Form the children into teams of two. Have one member be in charge of a rhythm instrument and create a fast or slow beat. The other member should choose a prop and mimic the tempo while using the prop in some way.

*Read a book slowly
Bounce a ball fast.
Mix some batter slowly.
Jump a rope fast.*

For an advanced project do an activity without props and have the member make up and pantomime it for the rest of the group to guess.

Fast

*Riding a bicycle
Chasing something
Racing a car or horse*

Slow

*Raking leaves
Carrying a tray full of food or glass full of milk
Fishing
Sewing on a button*

• Animal Walk

Bring in pictures of various animals to show the children. Discuss with them the ways each animal moves.

Play the varying tempos—slow, medium and fast in succession—while the children mimic the rhythm of each tempo in the guise of appropriate animals.

Slow—*Turtle, duck, snail*

Medium—*Goat, cat, elephant*

Fast—*Cheetah, deer*

After the children are familiar with the basic tempos, divide the class into three groups to represent the three tempos. Let each group agree on one animal to represent their tempo. Designate an area in the room for each animal group's home. Or, three large tables could be used for the animal groups to live under. You could set the mood by pretending they are in a lush jungle, busy barnyard or other setting appropriate to the animals.

When the leader plays a slow rhythm, the slow animals should all come out of their space or table house and move slowly in any way they wish around the room until the music stops, then return to their home base. Repeat the procedure with the medium and fast animal groups.

Expand the basic concept by having the children identify with other things that have similar tempos.

Slow—*A very old person, seaweed under water, snail or freight train*

Medium—*Falling rain, bees collecting honey or child riding a bike*

Fast—*Superman, lightning or jet plane.*

• If You're Happy. . .

This activity centers around the popular and lively song "If You're Happy and You Know It." It is a simple activity with an uplifting effect. Begin by asking the children what they do sometimes to show that they are really happy. (hug someone, jump in the air, shout) Let children take turns being leader by choosing their own ending of the song (spin around three times, hug someone, shout "yea, yea!," etc.). Then the class should immediately join in the action.

• Knees and Toes

This activity helps release tension, familiarizes the children with parts of the body, and is particularly useful for hyperactive children.

Either the instructor or one of the children may be leader, calling out the names of body parts to the group. The leadership can be rotated through the group.

If Bodi-Puppets are worn, parts are pointed out on the puppets rather than the children's own bodies so it is necessary that the puppets have several similar features.

The leader stands in front, facing the group, calling out (not demonstrating) the names of body parts. The group responds by putting both hands on that part of the puppet's body. Start with one feature at a time (head, shoulders, knees) and move to more complex combinations (head and knees; knees and toes; head, shoulders, knees and toes; turn yourself around, etc.). Each part mentioned is to be touched in order by both hands. Repeat exercise with another leader who will probably call out body parts in a different order.

• Mirror Game

This is a popular movement excercise that children find a challenging game for working in teams.

—*Form the children into teams of two.*

—*One child should act as the Mirror while the other is looking into the mirror.*

—*In a standing or seated position the looking child should very slowly begin to make movements for the mirror child to copy, exactly, just as a real mirror behaves. Continue for several minutes then let the children switch roles.*

The learning disabled child may find difficulty with this activity; in which case, this child may wish to stand behind his partner.

• Copy Cat

This activity teaches response and group rhythm. Ask the children if they know what the words "Copy Cat" mean. The teacher or a child may play the leader and demonstrate various actions for the children to mimic and copy as a group.

The leader should begin at one end of a room and perform only one hand or body movement while walking to the opposite end of the space, repeating the movement as many times as possible before reaching the opposite wall. The children should follow, one at a time, duplicating the movement as exactly as possible. If space permits, the entire group may follow the leader in unison.

Repeat the process using other ambulatory actions such as running, skipping, crawling, leaping or hopping.

Let another child have a turn playing the leader.

Children may wish to make Bodi-Puppets of cats to use in this activity and become cats for "Copy Cat."

• Amazing Spines

Children are intrigued by the inner workings of the body. The spine, as the body's major support system, can be made fascinating through creative movement activities.

Show a picture of a spine to the children and discuss the importance of spines with them. Ask the children what some of the things they can do with their spines are.

—*Touch toes.*

—*Be a Jumping Jack.*

—*Twist waist back and forth.*

—*Twirl around.*

—*Bend backwards.*

—*Hump back over like a camel.*

Then discuss with the children where the movement is originated in their bodies. Ask them to feel the spine from top to bottom of a classmate. How wide is is? What is it made of? What does it feel like?

Have each child make a bag Bodi-Puppet of a back

view of a character and draw a spine up the center of the puppet's back. The puppet can be worn on the back of the child, rather than the front to show how the spine flexes when the body moves.

• **Dragon Dance**

Response to sound and a sense of group rhythm are taught by the changing patterns of this dragon's dance.

Assign one child to play the Lead Dragon.

—*Have all the children and the Lead Dragon form a circle facing in one direction and move in a line while holding each other's waists.*

—*Beat a sound rhythm while the children move their feet to the tempo.*

—*Call the name "Dragon" as a cue for the Lead Dragon to break away from the circle while the rest of the children follow, making a* **linear** *formation.*

—*Continue to beat the sound rhythm and again call out "Dragon" while simultaneously tapping a child in the middle of the line to cue that child to break away from the original line. In doing so, this child becomes another Lead Dragon, forming a second smaller linear group behind him.*

—*Repeat the process as many times as needed until each child is moving by himself as a dragon.*

—*Reverse the procedure and merge the children, beginning with two children joining, then four, etc. until all are together and form one large dragon in the main circle again.*

Bodi-Puppets or exciting paper plate masks would both be fun to explore with this activity.

Dragon

• **Earth Element Dance**

This activity involves the group in a rhythm excercise that also helps the children learn to respond to sound. The children are divided into four groups representing Earth, Air, Fire and Water which the early Greeks believed composed all matter.

Briefly discuss these elements and ask the group to describe the characteristics of each. What does it feel or look like? (hot, cold, invisible) Why is it important?

—*Divide the class into four element groups.*

Designate an area in the room for each of the four elements. These areas could be color coded with tape or paper. For example: red for Fire, blue for Water, white for Air and brown for Earth. If you wish, pin matching color codes on the children who represent the four element groups.

—*Ask all of the children to form a large circle and hold hands while dancing in one direction. Tape a large "X" on the floor in one spot along the large circle pattern to signify the "breaking off" point.*

—*Beat a sound sequence such as 1-2-3-4; 1-2-3-4 as the children dance around the circle.*

—*Call out one element; for example, "Fire." The first child who represents Fire and steps over the "X" should break away from the large circle and go to the area in the room designated for Fire, forming a new smaller dance circle.*

—*The process is repeated as other elements are called and children go to their designated areas in the room.*

—*Continue until there is no one left dancing in the large circle and the four small element circles are completely formed.*

—*Reverse the procedure by calling the elements again and have each element go back to reform the large circle. (Be sure to mark each small circle with an "X.")*

—*Children may wish to create simple body pictures to represent each element to pin onto the front of their bodies. For example, waves or a fish could represent Water, clouds or birds the Air.*

• **Tension Release**

This activity will give the children an opportunity to learn to relax their bodies while releasing built up tensions. It is ex lent to do after a particularly tense work session.

—Children lie flat on the floor.

—Beat a sound for eight counts while the children tighten their muscles gradually (until they are as tight as they can get).

—Prompt the children during the beats by saying, "Tighter, tighter!"

—Beat a sound for four counts while the children completely relax.

—Repeat the excercise several times.

An expansion of the tension release exercises is to have children tense their entire body in a standing position and perform an activity while tense such as walking, running or hopping. Follow this up by having them relax their bodies and become floppy Raggedy Ann or Andy dolls.

These tension release exercises are particularly beneficial to the hyperactive child who may hold back a lot of tension.

● **Reach for a Star**

The following excercises are designed to wake the body, enliven it and build good muscle tone.

Have the children lie on the floor. Ask them to pretend that they are reaching out to touch a star. Begin with one arm.

— Tell the children to stretch way up. Because the star is very high in the sky, encourage them to stretch even more.

— Have them imagine that their arms are growing longer and longer. When each child has fully extended his arm, he can bring it down to the side of his body.

— Relax and repeat the process with the other arm.

— Follow this up with each leg and finally the entire body. The exercise can be repeated first in a sitting up, then a standing position.

— Finish by drawing the body into itself, curling up like a ball.

Now that they have touched a star, ask each to make a wish to share with the group.

Exploring and Developing the Senses

Most disabled children will not have use of one or more of their senses. Oftentimes this is due to the sense being "shut down" because of a handicap. Instead, the disabled child will place more emphasis on an existing, stronger sense and be able to develop it into special potential. It is important, however, to give as much opportunity as possible to each child in strengthening the undeveloped senses. The following activities are built around giving extra support in these areas.

● **Dance Tempo**

This simple loosening up activity helps children develop finer listening skills. Enliven the activity by using different types of instruments and music for the various rhythms.

Let the children dance or about freely about the space to musical patterns. When the music begins, the children should follow the music by moving to the tempo or style of the sound. When the music is stopped, the children should also stop or "freeze" in a stationary position. Repeat the procedure with a different music pattern.

A selection of records with a wide rhythm and tonal range—instrumental, orchestral or vocal arrangments—are fun to try and will encourage the children to listen carefully and match their movements to the music.

● **Drum Talk**

Introduce this activity by telling the class that drums have been used in many parts of the world to send messages from one place to another. Suggest that the class think of some warning that might be sent from one African village to another and decide upon the rhythm to convey that message. A very slow beat of five counts could mean a leopard is stalking nearby, or two fast beats, repeated, could signify a fire in the forest. The following excercise works out several communications using different rhythms and then suits movements to the drum's messages.

As drummer, the teacher should decide on a beat pattern or tempo to play and state a corresponding movement that the group should follow as the sound is played. For example:

Four slow beats — *The group should move in a straight line.*

Two fast beats — *They must do a sharp, about face.*

These two simple patterns may be repeated for a while, then new patterns introduced until a whole series of movements is established. The complexity of the series depends on the level of the children involved.

For an expanded activity, the beat patterns could be used to signify specific characters in actions, such as:

Four slow beats — *Tiger stalking*

Two fast beats — *Rabbit hopping*

Six slow beats — *Monster creeping*

Ten fast beats — *Child jumping rope.*

Children will also enjoy taking turns as leader and creating their own drum patterns.

• The Band

Children will learn to discriminate between different types of sounds in this activity as various instruments are brought into play. If the group is large, the teacher may wish to assign several children to be "The Band" and play the instruments.

Gather a variety of instruments (at least three), either homemade or real. Line them up and let the children look at them as they hear the sound each instrument makes. Then assign a specific movement direction to accompany each sound.

Xylophone — *Move forward.*

Drum — *Turn around.*

Wood blocks — *Hop on one foot.*

The leader should begin the exercise by choosing one instrument while the children respond with the proper movement. The leader then should switch instruments as the activity progresses and the children match it with the preassigned movements. Children will enjoy exploring a wide miscellany of sounds and movements in this manner, or even inventing their own actions.

If a group of children serves as the band, the teacher may simply conduct the band by tapping or pointing to each child when a sound is desired.

This is an excellent carry over to integrate into a story presentation using sound and movement such as the classic interpretation of "Peter and the Wolf."

Physically handicapped children can participate in band activity by having them perform the actions in a fixed position. Instead of moving about the room, they may be asked to move isolated parts of the body.

• Count the Beats

This exercise will help sharpen the children's listening skills as they count out the number of beats. The object is to tune the children into the beats so they learn to respond immediately when the sound stops. The leader plays distinctive beat patterns on a drum or box.

> —*Play eight beats, four times, while the children move freely about the space.*

> —*Make a definite pause at the end of the repeated beat series to signify that the children must "freeze." (Remain stationary in their positions.)*

> —*Repeat the procedure using only six beats (again play the beat series four times).*

> —*Repeat and decrease to four beats and finally two beats.*

When the children are familiar with the patterns, consider uniting the sets of beats into various combinations, rather than in a normal decreasing or increasing order. For example, you can play a series of eight beats, six beats, two beats, then four beats.

Variations can also be made on the style in which the children move. Instead of free movement, children may be asked to move only in curved lines, straight lines, quickly, slowly, or close to the ground.

Physically handicapped children can perform the activity sitting or lying down using only the upper or lower parts of their bodies.

• Rainbow Dance

This activity explores the spectrum of colors. Discuss with the children their favorite colors. Ask them have they ever seen a rainbow before? What colors are in rainbows?

> —*Let each child choose a color. Then draw something that represents that color on a sheet of paper. For example: Red could be represented by a rose, lipstick, fire engine or embarrassed face.*

> —*Pin the picture onto the child.*

> —*Have each child present a rainbow dance while wearing the picture. The dance or mime could evolve from the color picture or could be an expression of the child's own choosing.*

• Color Code

This is an enjoyable way for children to create patterns of rhythm with a color coded system and aid those who have trouble hearing or distinguishing tempos.

> —*Choose three colors to represent the three tempos, such as red for fast, yellow for medium, and green for slow.*

> —*Cut a number of 4 inch circle or square markers from each of these colors.*

—*Begin with one color only and lay out these color markers along the floor.*

—*Clap or beat out the tempo matching that color as each child moves from marker to marker, walking out the rhythm as if on stepping stones, one step for each colored paper marker.*

—*After one color has been introduced, try each of the other colors, separately.*

—*After all the children are familiarized with the colors and corresponding tempos, try combining the colors. For example: Lay out five red markers, ten green and three yellow in succession. This way the activity can be repeated with changing tempos.*

The children will enjoy making up their own rhythm patterns by laying out the colored pieces on the floor themselves and clapping out the pattern for the group to follow. Shapes and numbers can also be explored in this fashion.

● **Shape Dance**

An association between visual shape and movement is the object of this activity. It also introduces children to geometry.

—*Give each team of children a cardboard or paper geometric shape—triangle, square, circle or rectangle—all at least 18 inches across.*

Shape

—*One child should draw a line across the shape. It can be wiggly, zig-zagged, curved or other.*

—*The other child cuts along the line thus forming two shapes.*

—*Staple a ribbon strip or cord onto the top of each shape and tie one shape to each child (anywhere on the body that the child chooses).*

—*As a warm up, have each child take a turn moving freely with her shape about the space. Each shape should suggest to the child wearing it a certain movement pattern.*

—*Now play some music and let all children dance independently until the end of the music. At that time the children whose shapes match should end the dance so that their initial geometric shape is put back together.*

● **Poses**

Children will learn to observe clearly the details of a particular picture in this activity. It also introduces children to artistic works.

—*Bring in some paintings or magazine pictures of people such as athletes, dancers, actors and non-professionals shown in various poses for the children to study.*

—*Let each child select a picture and try to strike the same pose.*

—*The rest of the group can mimic the lead child's pose.*

—*Each child can then take a turn being leader.*

For blind children a pose may be verbally described by the leader for the child to perform, or sculpture may be explored.

Understanding and Expressing Language Through the Body

Some special children have difficulty understanding particular language concepts or in expressing the language they have inside. The following activities are designed to assist the child in discovering language through body movement and expression. A simple word concept can be better internalized through the action of doing, seeing, and experiencing. These provide the child with a motivating framework for learning. The activities rest on the premise of taking the conventional form of teaching in a two-dimensional plane and transforming it into a three-dimensional total experience, in an enjoyable setting.

- **Body Letters and Numbers**

Number and letter recognition can be reinforced through such activities as this which give three-dimensionality to printed concepts.

— *Have the children practice writing letters or numbers in the air with their fingers.*

— *Ask a child to write a particular letter or number in the air for the class to guess.*

— *Follow this idea up by letting the children write another letter, now using the entire body.*

Whole-body letters and numbers can be made by teams either standing up or lying on the floor. Four children can form the letters *M* or *W*. Two children can form the letters *L* or *T*. Challenge the class to form as many letters and numbers as they can. When all letters have been formed the instructor may direct the class to "start at the top" and form the letters in sequence from *A* to *Z*. *Bodi-pictures of letters may be attached to the front of children. Geometric shapes can also be explored in the same manner.*

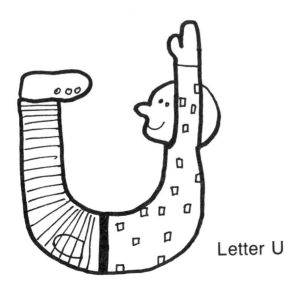

Letter U

- **Abstract Figures**

Responding to a line or shape is a fascinating activity that will challenge more advance students. After a little practice they can design their own figures and choreography.

— *Draw an interesting, but simple figure, on the blackboard, such as an S or U shape, or a swiggle or zigzag line.*

— *Ask the children to move across the floor while duplicating the same pattern (very much like skaters do for the Figure 8).*

— *Now let each child have a turn at drawing a figure on the board or piece of paper for the group to follow.*

— *After simple lines have been explored, try some more complex shapes.*

— *Partners may also draw figures for one another to follow.*

A group project can be done with each member drawing one simple figure on a long sheet of mural paper. This figure will indicate where the member will move in relationship to others in the group. Each child should use a different color when drawing the figure for easy discrimination. The group can then perform the series of figures in sequence, making up a total pattern of movements. Some of the movements may be repeated several times to lengthen and give variety to the patterning.

Consider playing some music and adding tempo to the project.

This project may also be done in reverse. The movement may be performed first by the teacher or a child and the group asked to draw the figure afterwards.

The mentally retarded child may be asked to follow a string figure laid out on the floor, instead of drawing a figure image on paper.

- **Moving Words**

The sounds of some words can strongly suggest their meaning. Such onomatopoetic words are the base for this activity.

— *Ask for contributions to a list of words that sound like their meaning.*

  growl   boom   hiss   cuckoo
  roar   buzz   ouch   ssh

— *Present the words one at a time asking the children to demonstrate the word by motion (no sound.) Be sure to include facial expressions as well as gestures.*

If words are written on the chalkboard as the list is made and referred to before and after the descriptive movement, the enactment of the word can be associated with its meaning and spelling.

• Opposite Actions

This exercise focuses the child's attention on the leader and promotes quick reactions to changing situations.

Discuss with the children beforehand opposite action words such as up/down; right/left; cry/laugh. Stand in front of the group and perform **one** action for the group, while they respond with the opposite action.

—*Look up/Look down.*

—*Move to the right/Move to the left.*

—*Touch toe/Touch head.*

—*Run fast/Run slow.*

—*Cry/Laugh.*

—*Put a pencil down/Pick a pencil up.*

The children will also enjoy exploring opposite words working in teams of two. One child leads while the other performs the opposite actions. Switch roles.

In addition to opposite action, the teams can create opposite characters. Have the children draw or cut out character images from magazines to attach to their bodies such as old person/baby, something ugly/beautiful (bulldog/butterfly). Afterwards the children can dramatize their characters with movements typical of the illustration.

For blind students, verbally describe the action and have them perform opposite actions.

• Nursery Rhymes

Nursery rhymes offer the opportunity for repetition in interpretations while reinforcing learning. They are also simple to perform and familiar to many children.

—*Read some of the rhymes to the group beforehand, and take time to show them illustrations. Find books with particularly appealing illustrations to share with the group.*

—*Have each child draw a picture of a nursery rhyme character that she would like to portray on a sheet of paper.*

—*Each child can wear the character picture while enacting the rhyme to the group. Other children may want to help in providing sound effects, such as "baaa" for a sheep, or a "thud" for Humpty Dumpty's fall.*

• As if. . .

Children will quickly grasp the concept of body language in this activity. Discuss with children that different experiences and emotions often affect the way a person moves. See if they can come up with a few starter examples, such as a sad person moving slowly across the room, with head hanging and shoulders sloping down. Then have the children go through the following emotions and situations.

Walking, as if: *Happy, tired, proud, embarrassed, in a cold storm*

Running, as if: *Afraid (a bear is chasing you), concentrating (trying to win a race), worried (being late to catch the school bus)*

Jumping, as if: *Joyful, pained (on hot sand)*

Sitting, as if: *Frightened, bored, uncomfortable (riding in a bumpy bus)*

Children may wish to extend the basic emotion idea into a fuller episode portrayal. For example, "Why are you walking proudly?" "Why is a bear chasing you?"

• Object Talk

Objects found around the house can be inspirational in developing story skits. Make a search for some interesting items or ask each child to bring in a special item to share with the group: wire whisk, hammer, ball, bag of nuts, sponge, perfume bottle, etc.

—*Arrange the objects on a table and let each child choose one object.*

—*Let the children take turns presenting a short activity using the object such as building something with the hammer, purchasing a bag of nuts, etc.*

Advance level students may work in pairs in developing complete skits around the object.

Also objects that could suggest several functions, such as a cardboard tube, cardboard disc, empty cereal box and pull apart L'Egg hosiery containers may be explored as focus for story skits. These objects can become many things according to individual whim. For example: The tube can be a telescope, rocketship or horn.

• People Patter

This activity will help children to build simple story skills by focusing on characterization.

Have the children perform the actions of a character with a specific career for the other children to guess. You may wish to list the names of the characters beforehand on flash cards to give the children.

- *Car Mechanic*
- *Typist*
- *Fireperson*
- *Farmer*
- *House builder*
- *Zookeeper*
- *Pizza chef*

• **Watch Me!**

This pantomime activity will help children to learn to observe more carefully the actions of another person. Also, recall is brought into play as each takes a turn mimicking the actions.

Choose a child to be the leader and give him the written or oral instructions for a short skit with a series of simple actions in sequence. Examples:

The Apple Tree

- *Walk down a country road.*
- *Climb a tree.*
- *Pick an apple.*
- *Climb down the tree.*
- *Walk away while eating the apple.*

• **The Great Swim**

- *Ride a bicycle to the beach.*
- *Get off the bicycle.*
- *Jump into the water.*
- *Swim around joyfully.*
- *Come out of the water.*
- *Dry off briskly with a towel.*

The child performs the skit in pantomime for a second child while all others in the class have their backs turned. The second child does the skit for a third, and so on. The process is repeated until all the children have seen the performance. The last child repeats the skit for the whole class which will enjoy seeing how much change has taken place between the first version and the last.

Children may be asked to help design their own skits as a Language Arts project.

• **Challenging Charades**

In this pantomime excercise children are encouraged to extend their acting skills creatively by doing a charade of some activity.

Give each child a short task to perform. Maintain secrecy by writing the task on a piece of paper or whispering the task in the child's ear. Or, children can draw out the written charade from a paper bag or box. Each child then performs her assigned task for the group to guess. Examples:

- *Riding a skateboard in a race.*
- *Playing a video game.*
- *Opening a hugh package and finding a bike.*
- *Planting a garden.*
- *Building a campfire and cooking a hot dog.*

Books on Dance, Rhythm and Music

Be a Frog, a Bird or a Tree: Creative Yoga Exercises for Children. Rachel E. Carr. Doubleday. New York, 1973.

Beyond Words. Elizabeth McKim and Judith Steinbergh. Holt, Reinhart and Winston. 1977. Two visiting artists collaborate to describe their teaching styles using sound/movement stories with special need children.

Creative Rhythmic Movement: Boys and Girls Dancing. Gladys Fleming. Prentice Hall. Englewood Cliffs NJ. 1976.

Dance Away! George Shannon. Illus. by Jose Arnego and Ariane Dewey. Wm. Morrow & Co., Inc. New York, 1982. For grades K-3.

Dance in the Desert. Madeleine L'Engle. Ill. by Symeon Shimon. Farrar, Straus, and Giraux, Inc. New York, 1969. For grades 4 and up.

Dance of the Animals. Pura Belpre. Ill. by Paul Goldone. Warne, Frederick and Co., Inc. New York, 1972. For grades 1-3.

Dance on the Dusty Earth. Christine Price. Scribner's, Charles and Sons. New York, 1979. For grades 4 and up.

Dancing Games for Children of All Ages. Esther L. Nelson. Sterling Publ. Co., Inc. New York, 1973. For grades 2 and up.

Dancing Tigers. Russell Hoban. Ill. by David Gentleman. Chatts-Bodley-Jonathon. Lawrence MA, 1980. For grades K-3.

Dancing Turtle. Maggie Duff. Ill. by Maria Horvath. Macmillan Publ. Co., Inc. New York, 1981. For grades K-3.

I Can Dance. Brian Bullard and David Charlsen. G.P. Putnam's Sons. 1979. A charming book with many photographs that gives simple basic ballet and yoga style dance steps.

Movement and Health Publications. Bill Stinson. Write to Div. HPER&A. Emporia State University. Emporia KS 66801.
To Move To Learn To Grow. A wide variety of move-

ment activities and experiences for young children (preschool through grade 3): movement exploration, creative exercises, simple rhythms, cooperative games, home-made equipment, perceptual-motor activities, and limited-space activities.

Fingers N' Hands in Motion. A comprehensive collection of fingerplays for the enhancement of a young child's hand-finger muscle development, eye-hand coordination, body part identification, and emotional control. The fingerplays have been organized into sections entitled: Me and Myself; People We Know; Toys, Things and Places; Special Days; The Seasons and Nature; and Animals.

When I'm Happy I'm Healthy. Contains "hands on" health educational activities for special children. For use with preschool and mentally retarded children of a cognitive functioning level comparable to primary grade levels (K-2). Includes: mental/emotional health, five body senses, body hygiene, personal appearance, accident prevention, comunicable diseases, nutrition, physical growth and fitness and dental health.

Musical Games for Children of all Ages. Esther Nelson. Sterling. New York, 1976.

Rhythms, Music and Instruments to Make. John and Martha Faulhaber, A. Whitman. Niles IL, 1970. Grades 3 and up.

Sally Go Around the Sun. Edith Fowle. Musical Arrangements by Keith MacMillan. Illus. by Carlos Marchiori. McClelland and Stewart Ltd. 1969. A vividly illustrated book on many popular songs and finger games geared towards active participation by children.

Silent Dancer. Bruce Hibok. Simon and Schuster. New York, 1981.

Singing and Dancing Games for the Very Young. Esther L. Nelson. Sterling. New York, 1977.

Sometimes I Dance Mountains. Byrd Baylor. Scribner's Sons. New York, 1973. Emotions and objects are expressed by a dancer's movements.

Teaching Creative Movement. Johanna Exuner and Phyllis Lloyd. Boston, 1974. Plays.

Books on Creative Dramatics and Mime

Clowns for Circus and Stage. Mark Stolzenberg. Sterling Pub. Co. New York, 1981. An excellent clown book that is filled with delightful photographs of clowns in mime activities.

Creative Dramatics and the Classroom Teacher. Ruth Heinig and Lydia Stillwell. Prentice Hall. 1974. A very detailed explanation of creative dramatics techniques. Especially valuable because of the extensive annotated bibliographies of materials suitable for pantomime, dialogue scenes, and story dramatization.

Development Through Drama. Brian Way. Humanities Press. 1967. A thorough discussion of drama in education. A thorough discussion of drama in education. Way stresses the use of drama in the development of the whole child. Of special interest to storytellers are: Chapter 3, "Begin from where you are" which describes how to in-

volve children in sound stories using an arrow for control; and Chapter 4, "Imagination" which discusses how to use stories and sounds to stimulate children's use of their imagination. A *must* for anyone interested in the educational use of drama.

Picture That! Bernice Wells Carlson, Abingdon Press. 1977. A collection of folktales from around the world. Each story is introduced with a related dramatic activity and followed by an art project. The author also describes how to present these types of activities to children. Also by the same author, **Let's Pretend It Happened To You.**

Puppetry and Creative Dramatics in Storytelling. Connie Champlin. Ill. by Nancy Renfro. Nancy Renfro Studios. 1980. A clearly written book with fresh ideas for the teacher who wishes to use puppets and creative dramatics to stimulate interest in children's literature. Fairy tales as well as modern favorites are used as examples.

Push Back the Desks, Albert Cullum. Citation Press. 1967. How Mr. Cullum integrated creative drama principles into his classroom teaching is the subject of this title. Of particular interest are the chapters dealing with, "Book Blabs," "Poetry Pot," and "Hallway Hoofbeats." Also, by the same author, **Aesop in the Afternoon** and **Shake Hands With Shakespeare.**

Seven Sound and Motion Stories. Joanna H. Kraus. New Plays for Children. 1971. Seven sound and action stories that can be used as independent dramatic activities or form the basis of creative dramatics sessions. Contains both traditional and modern stories.

Smiles, Nods, and Pauses. Dorothy Grant Hennings. Citation Press. 1974. Extensive collection of activities to enrich children's communication skills.

Story Songs. Carmino Ravosa. (Record) Omnisound. 1975. Sixteen songs based on favorite stories. Can be used as a basis for pantomime, to introduce characters or a story, and beginning dialogue. A charming record. Available from New Plays for Children, P.O. Box 273, Rowayton CT 06853.

Teaching With Creative Dramatics. June Cottrell. National Textbook Co. 1975. An excellent introduction to creative dramatics for anyone working with children. Bibliographies of stories to dramatize with various age groups are included. Storytellers will find the ideas for involving children in stories through sensory and pantomime experiences very useful.

Using Creative Dramatics Outside the Classroom. Roberta Nobleman. New Plays. New York, 1974. A small booklet of simple ideas to involve the children in creative dramatic skits with themes that children find appealing.

STORY PRESENTATION WITH THE SPECIAL CHILD

Texas School for the Deaf

By Nancy Renfro

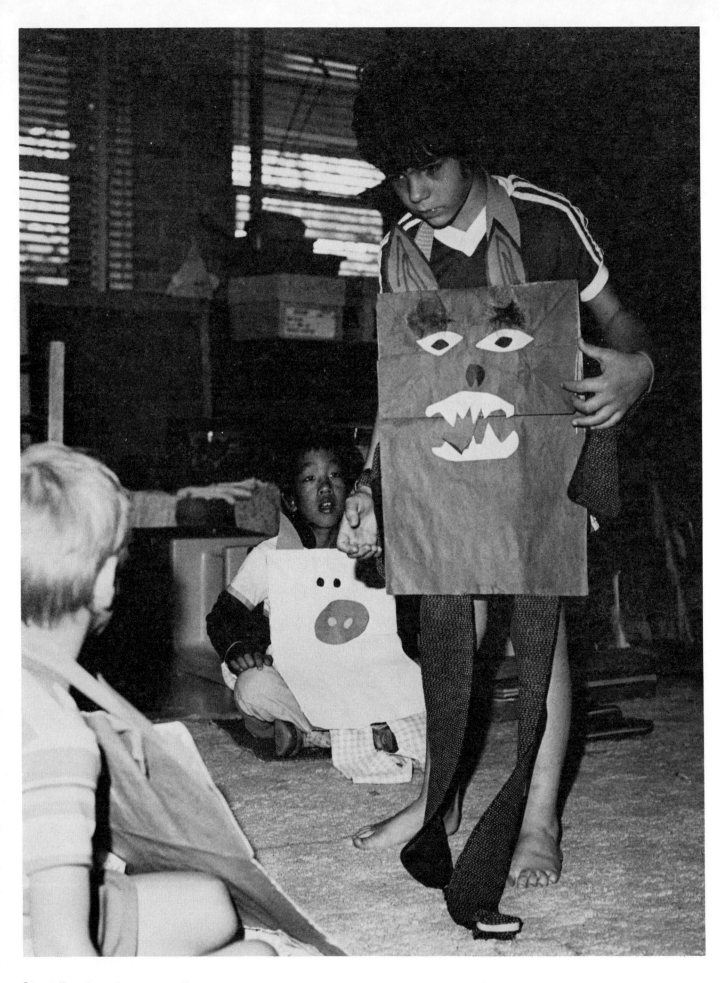

Storytelling through puppetry offers a means of expanding children's knowledge—*The Three Pigs Bag Bodi-Puppets*

Story Presentation with the Special Child

**The work of the Texas School
for the Deaf—Library**
By Nancy Renfro

Although a variety of approaches to storytelling have been investigated, few deal specifically with the unique needs of the special child. There is a spirit within each child, whether handicapped or not, that responds to a basic, elemental need to communicate. However, the special child must call upon specific inner resources within the limitations of a particular handicap for the communication and expression of ideas through the various senses. Storytelling through puppetry offers a means for exploring these inner resources while expanding the children's knowledge. The projects that follow were conducted at the Texas School for the Deaf during the various library sessions. This author was responsible for encouraging explorations with new puppet forms that were introduced in the course of several years' exploration within the library framework and staff members. The link between story presentation and puppetry became a strong focus in the library and resulted in children reaching new motivational levels in their desire to assimilate library material and understand language concepts. The benefits, in fact, were many.

There are several important precepts that children should learn about stories. By selecting a story and translating it into a puppet presentation, the teacher can present these precepts in an imaginative and fun-filled way. Using the puppet as a vehicle for expression is sometimes less complicated, less threatening than for the child to act with his own body. The puppet succeeds in diverting attention away from the child and puts him at ease in performing.

- **Characters**

Explore the concept of characterization as each child chooses the character he wants to play, thus establishing the main characters of a story. To

49

authenticate the puppet's unique qualities, the child must first study the physical and emotional aspects of his chosen character, so that the puppet matches the character in personality and appearance. For example, while making a squirrel, Keith noticed that the two front teeth were always prominent in photographs of squirrels; consequently, the teeth became an outstanding physical characteristic of his puppet. The process by which the child perceives the character is both creative and educational as the child learns to make judgments, studies personality development and translates observations into puppet action.

The child must analyze what the character says for content and meaning. What emotions does the character express? Why does it act in a certain manner? How does it relate to the story as a whole? Through dramatization, that is, the reliving of the story, a growing understanding evolves and can become internalized within the child.

• Vocabulary

The vocabulary in the story must be thoroughly understood for effective portrayal. Exploring the meanings of certain words and playing games of concentration are helpful in mastering the vocabulary in a given story. Improvisation and interpretations or even rewriting the story in the students' own words and using this rewritten script for the puppet presentation is an effective means of internalizing the story's language. In addition, the script itself makes an excellent reading exercise and review. Or, a script

Puppet presentation is an effective means of internalizing the story's language — *Goldilocks and the Three Bears String Puppets*

may not be needed at all if the story is read in a narrative style by the teacher or child directly from the book as the story is dramatized by the group with the puppets.

• Story Setting

The mood and setting of the story are essential factors to explore and make sure the children understand the contents. To successfully recreate the elements of story setting poses an artistic challenge to the class and offers the group a rich problem-solving situation. For example, "How would you create a happy mood? What colors would you use? How shall we create an ocean?" might be asked of the class to see how many ways and how expertly they can portray a particular setting or scenic suggestions.

• Sequencing

The sequence of events or scenes in a story and memory of the sequencing is necessary in presenting the story with puppets. Reviewing the story bit-by-bit, ordering the visual images and actions of the story in their proper order and making a miniature stage out of a cardboard box with paper stand-up figures for practicing the sequence prior to an actual puppet presentation are but a few of the ways to learn the order of actions.

The teacher might want to simplify this task by focusing on one or two of the previously discussed elements—the appearance of characters or certain scene settings, for example. The decision undoubtedly will be based on what areas of comprehension skills the teacher will want to explore and develop with individual students in understanding vocabulary, sequence, or other concept skills.

Presenting Stories With Puppets

Correlating art projects with the story presentation has tremendous value, especially with children whose deafness has given them a sharpened sense of visual perception. The integration of activities which the children can see and do is valuable in helping them better understand and visualize concepts and images in the story, something that might otherwise be very difficult to do. The story is not only enhanced visually, but puppets, with their ability to move, enliven the story by their very nature. In planning a story-puppet presentation with children who are hearing impaired, take the following points into consideration.

• Choose books with minimal dialogue and strong action. A story that can be primarily conveyed

through the actions of the puppets is preferred to one that depends solely on dialogue. Many of the classic fairy tales such as "Little Red Riding Hood" or "The Three Bears" are easily understood through the method of sequential pantomime. A modern counterpart can be found in Maurice Sendak's, *Where the Wild Things Are* in which action is continual and highly dramatic. On the other hand, a story such as Robert Kraus', *Leo the Late Bloomer* is a static one in terms of action, and relies mainly upon the narrative and whimsical illustrations for expressing its ideas.

• **Search out books with well illustrated imagery.** Stories that boast exciting graphics can be a bonus for working with the visually perceptive child. Byron Barton's, *The Airport*, is a fine example of bold use of color and shapes that children, expecially those who are visually impaired, will find exciting.

• **Choose puppet forms that allow suitable action or expression to complement the story.** With the wide selection of puppet types available, it is important to analyze those puppets that work well with specific books. The Bodi-Puppet, as shown in this section, is one of the few puppets which allows a child to sign words around the puppet's face and would be especially suitable for a story with dialogue that requires signing or intricate gestures. A Box Puppet, also shown in this section, is worn on the wrist and is more limited in expressing speech by a hearing impaired child. This type of puppet can, however, be quite effective in portraying a character of limited scope, like a bird or an insect that flits in and out of the story.

When presenting stories to children with disabilities, the story's messages and ideas are important, but the main focus must be placed upon whether or not the children are receiving the messages and assimilating the ideas. The entire group needs to be taken into account with the diverse concentration spans and comprehension levels considered. It would be wise to plan a program around a few short stories or a mixture of short stories combined with songs and poems, rather than one long story. Another solution would be to heighten interest by interspersing puppetmaking and creative dramatics with the story in

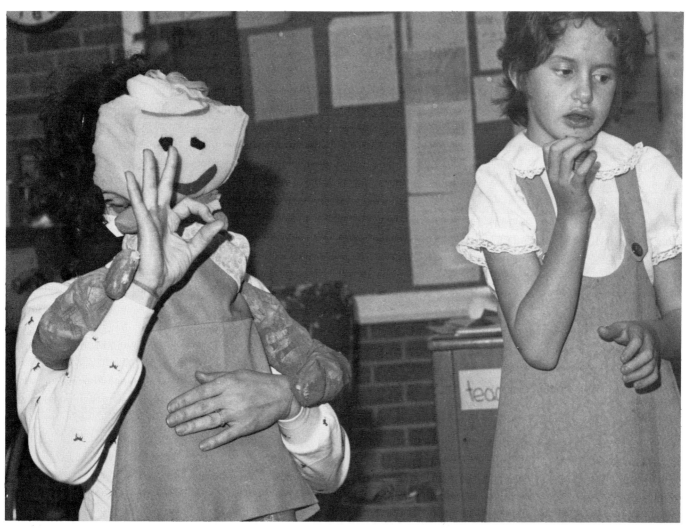

51

It is important to analyze those puppets that work well with specific books—*A teacher signs a story while wearing a Soft Foam Bodi-Puppet*

the program. Even when time is limited, this approach is possible, with children making instant Stick Puppets from magazine pictures or precut shapes attached to drinking straws, and mimicking the actions of the characters.

Let children participate in the story presentation itself, even if the involvement is minimal. Children who cannot hold a puppet because of poor muscle control can be asked to provide sound effects or even facial expressions (smile, frown, etc.) for the character. Holding up a prop such as a moon on a stick or providing musical accompaniment with a tapping drum or clanging triangle are other areas for participation. Children with more agility can take on the lead roles, but all the children can contribute by determining movements and dialogue.

Materials and Tools

Proper materials and tools are needed in puppetmaking activities when working with special children, but sensitivity to the children's fears or their limitations in using these items should also be considered. Some children will have no trouble working with common classroom materials—scissors, glue, paper, etc. Others might shy away from or even refuse to use certain items. A child who has a fear of scissors will not be able to be included in a puppetmaking project that requires cutting of paper. In this case, a substitute should be sought. Paper can easily be torn into shapes by the child, or precut shapes can be prepared beforehand by the teacher. In precutting puppet components such as eyes, noses, lips and other body parts, it is advisable to include enough variety so that the child has a rich selection from which to choose. Thus, there is a decision making process involved in building the puppet as the child choses whether to make the eyes round or squinted, or whether the mouth should be sad or happy. These experiences are side benefits when making puppets with the children and enhance the learning process. As a child observes classmates working with scissors, she may wish to try them on her own initiative. However, scissors or other tools should never be forced upon a child until the child is ready.

Decision making can also include the group as a whole as they create a puppet together. Starting with a basic form for the puppet's body, such as a stuffed paper bag or detergent box, the leader can direct the creation of the puppet's design by asking the children certain questions, i.e., what kind of arms, legs, ears, or other features the character might have. If children with limited motor skills cannot actually create the parts themselves, then the leader can construct them while following the children's directions. Or, simple geometric precut shapes can be on hand to

tack onto the box for facial features. As a child observes classmates working with scissors, for example, she may wish to try them on her own initiative. However, scissors or other tools should never forced upon a child until the child is ready.

All puppetmaking projects would benefit from materials having in stock some basic materials:

Brushes—small, medium, large sizes
Cardboard—posterboard, oak-tag
Coloring Media—pencils, crayons, felt-tipped pens, tempera paint, latex wall-paint
Construction Paper—assorted colors
Glue—white glue, glue sticks, rubber cement, paste
Scissors—blunt tipped
Stapler—desk and hand types
Tape—masking, cellophane

A good quality hand model stapler with a long nose, such as the Arrow P-22, is a worthwhile investment for aiding the leader in assembling puppets with children. It is a jam proof stapler with extra dexterity and stapling strength for cardboard as well as paper materials.

A selection of tools as part of work materials for children will offer opportunities to increase motor dexterity. Experiment with the different types of blunt-edge metal and plastic scissors to determine those best suited to the needs and abilities of the children. A holepunch is fun to have on hand since children enjoy the patterning which results from punching out a myriad of dots from a sheet of paper. A compass is useful for advanced students in drawing circles and a ruler for straight lines. Architectural supply stores carry a fascinating line of plastic templates with various geometric shapes that are excellent for tracing designs and features.

To the basic collection gather together an interesting variety of materials which offer rich sensory stimulation to the experience of puppet making, such as:

—*Aluminum foil*
—*Cotton or polyfiber*
—*Decorative trims*
—*Drinking straws*
—*Fabrics (burlap, shiny polyesters, felt, Pellon, muslin, wool, velours, corduroy, voile, etc.)*
—*Foam rubber*
—*Food boxes (egg carton, pudding, cereal and other boxes)*
—*Gift wrapping and holiday paper*
—*Gum stickers (stars, dots, rectangles)*
—*Ice cream wooden sticks*
—*Oaktag or file folder paper*
—*Paper cups*

—Paper fasteners
—Paper plates
—Pipe cleaners
—Plastic food wrap
—Quilting batting
—Rubber bands
—Sequins
—Sponges
—Styrofoam balls
—Wallpaper samples

You will soon discover which materials appeal to certain children and will want to continue to include these materials in future projects. Introduce new materials gradually so that the children will have time to experiment with each new item. If possible, keep a record of the specific materials and techniques that appeal to each child. One child might enjoy snipping paper while another finds the process of rubber cementing soft fabric scraps onto foam more fun. Increase these basic enjoyments by expanding and enriching the child's material repertoire. Remember that puppetmaking activities that take place prior to the story time establish a special bond between the child and story. This positive experience not only creates anticipation but provides a unique strengthening of the concepts in the story, a strengthening augmented by the use of puppets in the storytelling circle.

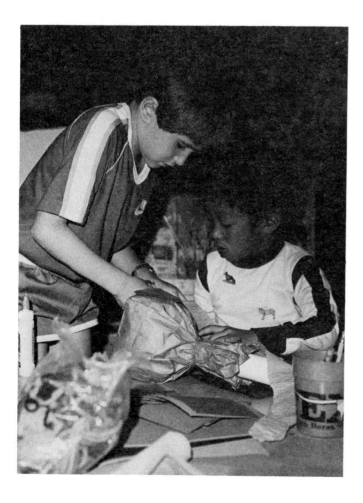

Planning the Program

Being open-minded as well as positive about progress taking place, no matter how minimal, is of utmost importance when working with the special child. Expectations should not be based upon general statistics but rather on the specific abilities of the individual child. A standard lesson plan may be referred to in preparing an activity in the school library, but invariably the actual plan must be altered when working with the children. Although it is important to have an outline with objectives when doing a puppet centered project, it is necessary that the teacher believes that the child is capable of learning. With this basic premise understood, empathy, patience and a willingness to let go of the planned lesson in order to meet the immediate needs of the children, even changing objectives midstream, are prerequisite to a successful story presentation. This does not necessarily mean that structure and planning should be discontinued, only that flexibility is critical; altering the planned course of action can lead to unexpected and sometimes significant improvements in a child's growth. For example, you have planned to teach the children the lyrics to "Old MacDonald Had a Farm" using animal puppets to parallel action. If the children express difficulty in retaining the words to the song, or cannot follow its fast pacing, a certain degree of fulfillment for the children can be achieved by having them, instead, learn the sounds of the animals. In a subsequent lesson, the sounds can be matched with the lyrics. Furthermore, adjusting the pace of the song to correspond with the children's ability will help in achieving goals and some measure of success.

In a similar vein, if a particular story is too complex for the children to grasp or participate in its entirety, trim the story down to is essential elements and let the children participate in key dialogue or actions. For example, in "Three Little Pigs," invite them to join in the refrain, "I'll huff, and I'll puff and I'll blow your house down!" each time the wolf threatens the little pigs. If a child cannot speak the words, then devise an action which she can mimic while others recite the words. Excellent activities for choral speaking and other simple participation approaches can be found in *Books, Puppets and The Mentally Retarded Student* by Jack and Connie Champlin.

The ideas that follow for presenting stories with puppet accompaniment are among the most successful ones tried in the Texas School for the Deaf library. The various groups of students, both deaf and multi-disabled children, attended class on a daily basis for a thirty minute period at the library. These successive short sessions provided an ideal opportunity for pup-

You will soon discover what materials appeal to certain children

pet story sessions since they gave ample time to break down a project into segments and to plan a variety of interrelated activities.

A typical segment which focuses on a particular story may stretch out over several sessions and include both puppetmaking activities and story presentation. The following is an example of a program outline based on the story *Octavius*, a delightful story by Betty Hubka about an octopus who changes colors when expressing emotions.

Session 1—**Introduce new vocabulary words..** Collect pictures and photographs of assorted fish and other ocean creatures, cut out pictures and put up on the bulletin board for comparison and study of sealife vocabulary. Afterwards, ask the children to draw pictures of their own fish. Note: *National Geographic, Ranger Rick*, and other photographic nature magazines make excellent source material and are readily available by donation.

Session 2—**Reinforce vocabulary.** A movie on octopi is shown to the group, followed by further discussion and new discoveries about the habitat and habits of the octopus.

Session 3—**Tell the story.** Having given the group an opportunity to assimilate vocabulary, read the story. For discussion, compare the sealife in the movie with the pictures on the bulletin board.

Session 4—**Create the puppets.** Ask the children to build dioramas of ocean environments in shoeboxes, using glue, construction paper, sand, shells, grasses, and other materials. The fish pictures on the bulletin board may be incorporated into dioramas to enhance the scenes. Each child makes a turn-around paper image of the lead character, Octavius, which is blue on one side and red on the other. Attach puppet to a drinking straw rod so that it can be maneuvered in a slit along the box's top.

Session 5—**Review the story.** The story is retold with the participation of the entire group. Each child is asked to dramatize one segment of the story using her storybox and lead puppet in sequential episodes. For example, one child can enact the scene in which Octavius turns blue when hiding; another child can dramatize the scared, red Octavius and still another can portray Octavius when he is being chased by a shark.

For the teacher who is unfamiliar with working with handicapped children, this dissection approach to a story is a reversal of the typical story presentation, in which the story is read first and related activities such as understanding vocabulary, and review follow. However, because deaf or multi-disabled students often have limited knowledge of the vocabulary in a new story, they may miss some of the content of the story. Therefore, it is recommended that time be spent first in analyzing the key words or concepts so that the story's full significance will reach the children. Each book will obviously vary in the words or concepts that need to be emphasized. In *Octavius*, the study focuses on sealife vocabulary, whereas a story such as "Goldilocks and The Three Bears" centers around the concept of size gradation.

The last session is devoted to story reinforcement and review. It is important that each child in some way participates in the story as it is retold with the puppet. If the story is short, then each child can tell the entire story with his own interpretation. A longer story such as *Octavius* requires other solutions because of the time factor. Letting each child tell *one* aspect of the story works well and involves many children while keeping presentation time to a reasonable length. Another solution is to let the children perform in unison, providing certain key words, sounds, or actions for the lead character, or joining in the refrain, if there is one.

The last session is devoted to story reinforcement and review. It is important that each child in some way participates in the story as it is retold with the puppet. If the story is short, then each child can tell the entire story with his own interpretation. A longer story such as *Octavius* requires other solutions because of the time factor. Letting each child tell *one* aspect of the story works well and involves many children while keeping presentation time to a reasonable length. Another solution is to let the children perform in unison, providing certain key words, sounds, or actions for the lead character, or joining in the refrain, if there is one.

Presentation Formats

The following ideas represent a few highly successful presentation formats or techniques that may be used with students in the library to present stories with puppets by children. The leader will soon discover which formats are most appropriate in linking up with available story books; the formats require a certain amount of preparation and time. However, if time is a limiting factor consider using the simple puppet ideas listed at the end of this chapter for improvised and quick presentations.

• Storyboxes

Storyboxes are actually a spinoff of the familiar shoebox dioramas used in many classrooms. However, they are carried one step further as the characters are animated within the context of the scenic display of the box. The storybox becomes a miniature theater which can be used by the teacher as a visual tool as the story unfolds, or as an artistic activity to help the children become acquainted with various story settings and characters.

The storybox has high motivational value in both enabling the students to learn the story while offering them a visual means of presenting the text. When the children manipulate the detailed set in accordance with the story, a tactile emphasis is given to the accompanying text, whether expressed verbally or in signed English. A major benefit of the storybox is that it provides ample opportunity to build vocabulary,

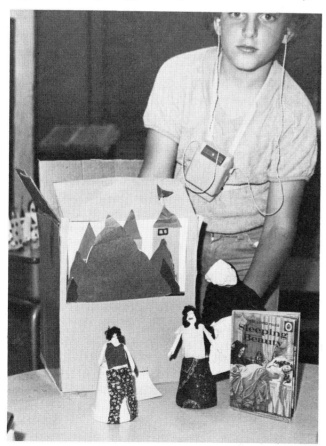

both collectively as a class and individually. Working with the children to determine a list of items that they would like to include in their storyboxes, such as *Drawbridge* for "Robin Hood," or *Porridge* for "The Three Bears," will add new words to enrich their ever expanding vocabulary. These words will be even more valuable to the children because the list evolved from their own experience. As students strive to think of details they might include in their individual storyboxes, they automatically review and recall the story; thus vocabulary and memory are enhanced.

In this project, a class of fifth grade hearing-impaired students, focused on books with classical themes. Each member spent time in the library searching for a book of particular interest to convert into a puppet presentation. The end result, of course, was that many new books would be shared by the group, rather than just one. The themes they chose were diverse—*Snow White and the Seven Dwarfs, Wizard of Oz, Sleeping Beauty* and a host of others.

Although the project, in its initial conception, was based upon the idea of making a shoebox diorama, the class deviated from the original plan in execution. First, grocery cartons were used instead of shoeboxes, providing a larger work space in which to build the set. Second, the box surfaces were used in any way that the student felt would be most effective for their chosen story. For example, in *Snow White*, the inside of the box represented the interior of the Seven Dwarf's house, while in *Robin Hood*, the outside was converted into a castle. The children's creative interpretations of the boxes were both exciting and varied. Sometimes the text suggested an idea that was then translated into physical terms, as in the *Wizard of Oz*. Here, the renowned and endless yellow road was illustrated on a paper scroll and placed on two rollers inside the box, to be rolled along as background scenery as small stand-up paper characters were activated in front of the set.

In choosing the props to include in the storyboxes, the children developed a skill for focusing on the essentials of a story. Since children with visual impairments or those who are multi-disabled may have difficulty recognizing the crucial elements of a story, the inclusion of specific details into these storybox dioramas provided the student with a clearer understanding of the whole picture.

The children spent time perusing their books, to glean the general content, from both the narrative and visual images presented. Then the librarians, working individually with each child, explored what elements in each book stood out as most important to the child. In the case of *Snow White* it was the seven little beds that Snow White tucks the dwarfs in. It was in this way that the basis for each storybox was

Sleeping Beauty Storybox with Stand-Up Puppets

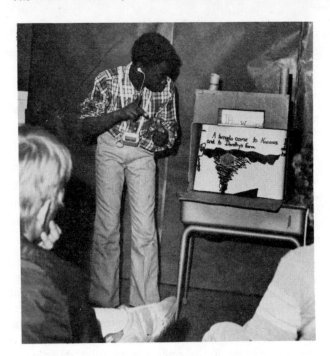

determined.

The rich assortment of materials used to create the details of the storyboxes was an important aspect of the project, in that it allowed the children to make new tactile discoveries and to make numerous decisions. Be sure to provide a wide selection of materials, both natural and synthetic, through which the children can rummage. Wallpaper samples can be used to line the walls of a house; brick contact paper makes an effective exterior or wall design. Plastic food wrap and aluminum foil are marvelous for windows or authenticating science fiction sets, and throwaways, such as egg cartons and small boxes, make excellent furnishings when cut to proper shapes. Don't overlook items from the natural environment—rocks, twigs and sand—which can realistically enhance an outdoor scene.

The puppets that the children created were as varied as the sets in which they were placed. There were no limitations placed as to which kind of puppet they were to make, and so, each child chose what he wished—Finger Puppets, Stick Puppets, Stand-up Puppets, Hand Puppets, even masks and costumes for life-size puppets. Sometimes a child would come up with a multi-media solution. A vivid example was the version of *Snow White and the Seven Dwarfs*, in which the Seven Dwarfs were depicted by paper Finger Puppets and Snow White, not a puppet at all, was portrayed by the child wearing a simple costume. By adding a tall, pointed paper cone hat to her basic costume the star portrayed the wicked queen as well. In the *Wizard of Oz*, the performer used small paper Stand-Up Puppets for Dorothy, the Scarecrow and the Tinman, but chose to play the Lion's role himself with only a small rag of fake fur thrown over his head. It was a very charming presentation as he wove in and out of the story's plot, providing growling sounds at appropriate points.

At the culmination of the project, the children were given an opportunity to practice by themselves before presenting their stories to the class. In addition each performer was videotaped by the school's media specialist, making the children feel quite important and proud of their end products. Furthermore, they were able to view their productions later, at leisure, and enjoyed them again.

The children presented in their final presentations an improvised, condensed version of their stories, using sign language and/or partial speech, to highlight the most dramatic episodes such as Snow White eating the poisoned apple. Since not all of a story's text was incorporated in the presentation, the general organization of the story was stressed. In this way, the students got a better appreciation of the story's sequencing, a language skill that is difficult for the hearing-impaired child.

The storybox project taught the children several aspects of language development—new vocabulary words, identification of the main theme of the story, sequencing and interpretation of the essence of the story. It proved to be one of the most successful projects of the school year, in terms of providing a total story experience. The words on a printed page became a three-dimensional production experience. A final outcome of the project was that each storybox since it was individually executed and self-contained, provided the performer with a moment of glory, as star, producer, director and focus of all attention by teacher and peers. Truly it was a moment to savor, and remember!

Table-Top Stories

The Table-Top Story is an expanded version of the Storybox method of presentation. The story's actions, rather than being confined to the limited setting of the box, take place upon the entire surface of a table or even a designated floor area. Tabletops are especially accessible to children in wheelchairs, since the table is an ideal work level for maneuvering or viewing the scenery and puppets. Even with children who are mobile, the tabletop allows great freedom in moving around the perimeter of the table to perform action. The puppet setting may be transferred to the floor area, especially for the ease and safety of children who have severe physcial handicaps and are more comfortable on the floor.

Many of the disabled children at the Texas School for the Deaf are restricted in experiencing new environments because of their severely limited mobility. The world that is famliar to them is limited to their school and home environments. With Table-Top settings, the children, especially those with physical limitations, are provided with opportunities to ex-

plore new environments—a productive farm, bustling city, noisy zoo or colorful ocean floor. Hopefully, there will be a way to actually get the children to some of these interesting places, but in any case, exposing them to the workings of the farm or the clamor of the city will enhance their experience and comprehension.

The kind of story that lends itself best to this form of puppetry has action which takes place in several locations, and the main character follows the action. The *Gingerbread Man*, for example, is ideal material for Table-Top interpretation since the lead character runs through diverse pathways while being chased by a host of other cast members before his culmination in the pond. *Airport* by Byron Barton is another well matched story for Table-Top play. This book is a good example of clearly illustrated information based on a technical theme. The airport's complex organization and how it functions is a fascinating subject to children as they learn how people arrive, check in baggage, purchase tickets, board flights as well as how the planes are serviced and depart. Replicas of the airport's various components will aid the children in dramatizing the story with Finger or Stand-Up Puppets. Airplanes, terminals and other key components can be built from cardboard tubes, food boxes and common throwaway items. Toy airplanes may also be mobilized.

For groups who are severely disabled, reality-based themes are especially appropriate to introduce through this technique. Exploring neighborhood en-

Table-Top Barnyard Scene

vironments would not only be interesting to the children, but would also help to build new relationships and an awareness of the neighborhood's composition. Such stories as Children's Television Workshop's *Who Are the People in Your Neighborhood?* are suitable material for neighborhood study. Layouts of houses, blocks, and roads, shopping complexes and community buildings give a basic background for this field trip in miniature.

The Table-Top setting can be assembled from an array of throw-away items. Styrofoam packaging and food boxes of assorted shapes make excellent buildings and vehicles. Cardboard tubes can be easily converted into trees with fringed paper foliage. To establish spatial relationships, consider making the ground of the set as a first activity with the children. This grid or other patterning can simply be strips of paper arranged on the table to represent sidewalks, roads or pathways, taped in place. A more elaborate groundscape could be painted or drawn on a sheet of mural paper, and easily resurrected for use at another time. Grassy green areas, swiggling rivers and other environmental markings can be added for detail. Items from nature such as stones, sand and dried grass add interesting touches, and can either be positioned or glued permanently in place.

Two types of puppets are suitable for Table-Top presentations—the Walking Finger Puppet or Stand-Up Puppet. Children who have finger dexterity will be intrigued with the Walking Finger Puppet concept, which can actually move the puppet through the story's actions. Little Red Riding Hood can follow a path through the woods or The Billy Goats Gruff can tramp over a cardboard bridge, using the child's fingers as the character's legs. A series of linear pathways drawn on the groundscape will provide the children with additional reinforcement of hand/eye coordination as they attempt to follow the lines with their fingers. A network of paper strip pathways taped to the floor can also be exciting, especially for children who are physically active and enjoy working in large areas.

Looking for Suzie by Bernadine Cook is an example of a story that makes good use of the larger space afforded by the floor. The various farm buildings in this story—the chicken coop, barn and hayloft—represented by various boxes are laid out in appropriate locations, and then linked together with a continuous sidewalk strip. The children who portray the lead characters go from place to place on the farm, searching for their lost cat, Suzie; as they proceed, the path takes them from building to building and finally terminates in the hayloft, where they discover that Suzie has just had a litter of kittens. The lead characters are portrayed by Walking Finger Puppets

while Suzie and her kittens can simply be paper cutouts because their role in the story is an inactive one. Groups of children from the class will enjoy taking turns in this search for Suzie; the story can be replayed a number of times with interest sustained by hiding the kittens in a different location each time the story is enacted.

Stand-Up Puppets are also suitable for Table-Top Stories. These puppets are particularly appropriate for children who have only limited agility in their fingers or for those children with no dexterity at all. If the puppet is placed directly in front of a child, the child can then participate by providing appropriate sounds or expressions for the puppet. The leader may assist in maneuvering the puppet to a different location, if that is necessary for the child. Stand-Up Puppets can be constructed from a cereal or detergent box to make a large puppet, or from a pudding box or similar sized box for a smaller puppet. Paper feet attached to the bottom of the box assure stability. Most commercially available hand puppets can also be converted into Stand-Up Puppets by placing them over weighted plastic bottles. With some ingenuity, stuffed toys, mechanical toys, doll and other ready-made items can also be utilized to portray characters in Table-Top stories.

Walking Finger Puppets

Materials: Greeting card, magazine picture drawing or photocopy of the character; oak tag, poster board, or stiff paper; and small rubber band.

Construction: Cut out the character's image and reinforce the picture by gluing it to a piece of poster board or stiff paper. Staple the rubber band across the lower back of the puppet as

rubber band

Witch

Stand Up Box Puppets

Materials: Pudding, cereal, detergent, milk carton, or other type box; construction paper; and scraps of fabric.

Construction: Attach paper features onto a box or glue the character image onto the front of a small pudding or cosmetic box. Add paper feet to the bottom of the box for extra stability.

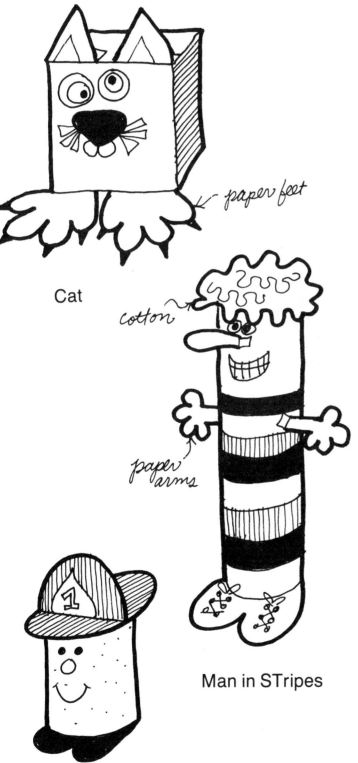

Cat

cotton

paper arms

paper feet

Man in STripes

Fireman

Bodi-Puppet Presentation

Most traditional puppets, especially those with talking mouths, are not well suited for working with deaf or hearing-impaired children. Because their speech is often inadequate, in terms of projection and pronunciation, these children must rely on someone else to speak or sign their puppet's dialogue, which means the puppets are quite limited in action and expression.

The Bodi-Puppet, a life-sized puppet worn in front of the child's body, is the perfect alternative. Supported by a neck ribbon, with elastic bands attaching the puppet's hands and legs to the puppeteer's wrists and ankles, the Bodi-Puppet still retains the properties of puppetry while allowing the hands to be free for signing and the mouth to be unobstructed for speech.

Although the child can be seen, as with Japanese Bunraku puppets (a traditional form of life sized puppets held in front of the body), the body does not detract from the puppet. It is as though the child becomes one with the puppet. Bodi-Puppets become an extension of the child. This medium also offers a unique opportunity for children with multi-handicaps to develop motor coordination and body awareness through activities involving creative dramatics.

Used in storytelling, these puppets offer special experiences. The large size of the Bodi-Puppet makes them more easily seen by a larger audience. In the process, their use expands the puppet stage to all available floor space and opens the way for more imaginative and creative movement. Furthermore, young children find the skillls of cutting and gluing materials onto large sized Bodi-Puppets more easily mastered than either sewing or gluing features onto the smaller more conventionally scaled creations.

A more realistic touch is added to the story by the use of full scale props, such as chairs and tables as well as more elaborate backdrops or painted murals. Because of their bold scale, these puppets are ideal for stage productions and outdoor activities.

In choosing appropriate stories for use with Bodi-Puppets, search out material with changing pace of action by the main characters. "The Shoemaker and the Elves" and "Hansel and Gretel" are two classics which, with simplification, lend themselves to this form of puppetry. Modern examples include Verna Aardema's, *Who's in Rabbit's Hole* and Byron Barton's, *Buzz, Buzz, Buzz.* The *Voyage of Jim* by Janet Barber was a highly successful theme presented by a fifth grade level class of deaf students at the library. The many characters illustrated in the book gave students colorful imagery for creating Bodi-Puppets through animal and sea life. Active songs, dances and games are also fun to explore with Bodi-Puppets. A basic collection of farm animals make up an excellent repertory cast for the many farm related songs such as the "Farmer in the Dell" and "Old McDonald had a Farm". The same cast can be used for *Henny Penny* and *Buzz, Buzz, Buzz* by Byron Barton. Children may wish to create a diversified set of characters of their own choosing to incorporate with popular songs as "Looby Loo," "Here We Go 'Round the Mulberry Bush" and "If You're Happy and You Know It." The puppets, of all shapes and descriptions, participate in a circle formation, while singing and acting out the songs.

The three basic Bodi-Puppet constructions used by the groups were the Paper Bag, Hosiery and Box and the Soft Foam Bodi-Puppet, for which instructions follow.

To Make Paper Bag Bodi-Puppet

This simple version of the Bodi-Puppet is the easiest of all to construct and the large paper bag which comprises the body is an excellent surface on which to glue, draw and paint. Children who are limited in their artistic abilities may simply wish to choose pictures from magazines, such as plants, vehicles, animals, or people to paste onto the bag's flap. This suggestive image will suffice to represent a character's role. Other children will wish to create their own features and decorative costuming to further define the character. Fabric strips for arms or wings, as in the case of birds, and a neck-ribbon completes the puppet. Strips may also be added for legs but are optional as the child's legs can easily serve as the puppet's legs walking, hopping and skipping through the story.

Materials: Large grocery bag; two medium rubber bands; two 3-inch wide fabric strips (length of the child's arm); 2½-foot long fabric strip or ribbon for securing around neck; construction paper; and scrap fabric and trims.

Construction: Fold over the end of each fabric-strip and slip a rubber band in each hem; staple hems to secure rubber bands. Staple other end of each arm strip to paper bag, just below flap. Staple center of ribbon to top center of bag. Use a rich assortment of materials and coloring medium to add character, pattern and texture to the bag. Tie neck ribbon around the child's neck and slip rubber bands over wrists. The child then "becomes" the puppet and can dance or pantomime actions using his own legs and the fabric-strip arms.

Lion

Goat

To Make Soft Foam Bodi-Puppets

These puppets made from a soft foam rubber material have a doll-like appearance. They are sturdy, soft and squeezable while looking suprisingly like real people. Children with multi-handicaps have found them particularly appealing and enjoy carrying them around or playing with them even when not engaged in storytelling activities. In a sense, they become the child's special friend, one with whom they experience security. You may even wish to include them in other activities in your curriculum.

Investing time in creating a basic sturdy puppet such as this one for each child in the group at the beginning of the school year is worthwhile. Once the puppet is completed, it can be used throughout the year with interchangeable props and costume modifications. A bonnet on the puppet's head makes a perfect Little Miss Muffet or Old Mother Hubbard, while floppy felt ears attached to the head will convert the puppet into a dog or rabbit. Search your local upholstery shops for scrap foam generally used to make cushions, or inquire at your nearby discount stores for purchasing large slabs of foam. A long blunt tipped saw-tooth bread knife is most efficient for cutting out the foam. "Saw" the block of foam as if it were wood. This step should be done by yourself, although the process can be accomplished by older students (5th grade and up) with normal manual dexterity, assuming an adult is closely supervising the activity.

Materials: Two pairs panty hose; 13 by 18 inch, 2 to 4 inch thick foam (obtained from upholstery store); newspapers; 3 by 36 inch soft fabric strip; felt scraps; yarn; and recycled clothing.

Construction: With a long blade saw tooth bread knife (adult use only) cut out a body shape following the basic dimensions below. (Do not be concerned if the shape appears somewhat jagged for children are noncritical of perfection.) Stuff hose legs with crumpled newspaper for limbs. Leave panty sections unstuffed. Attach one hose to neck area of puppet by knotting around neck of foam body. These are the arms. Attach second hose to puppet by slipping waist of hose up over bottom of foam puppet to puppet's waist. Staple hose waist area to foam in several places to secure. Tie fabric strip to back of knotted arm hose to serve as neck tie around child's neck. (The arms and legs of these puppets are not attached to the child.) The child should grasp the end of the arms with his hands and operate the puppet's arms in a free manner. The legs simply dangle down. Features and yarn or fringed felt hair can be added to puppets by gluing onto foam with rubber cement. Dress the puppets in recycled clothing.

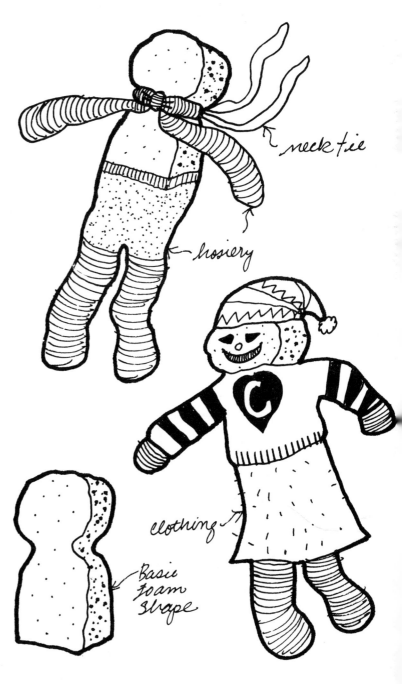

neck tie

hosiery

clothing

Basic foam shape

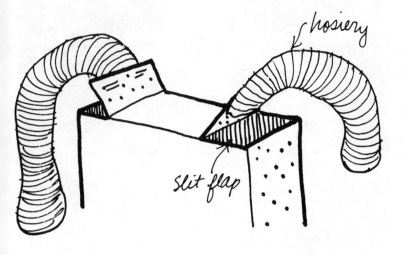

hosiery

slit flap

To Make Hosiery and Box Bodi-Puppet

This advanced Bodi-Puppet construction uses stuffed hosiery for arms and legs, and throwaway items for the remaining body components. A large detergent box or poster board cut to shape makes an excellent body; a paper plate or smaller box serves well for a head. Children will have a greater range of creative freedom if a rich assortment of materials are provided both for the basic puppet construction as well as the enhancement and detailing.

Egg cartons and cardboard tubes make intriguing features such as eyes and noses. Also consider recycling old clothing and actually dressing the puppets in real shirts, ties, hats and even jewelry to create an impressive effect. The crumpling of newspapers and actual stuffing of the hosiery to create limbs for the puppets is an excellent motor skill activity for children who have poor dexterity. The leader will need to give individual assistance to the students in assembling the puppets. Since these puppets will require a long time period for adequate completion, plan a series of short work sessions so as not to tax the children's stamina or capabilities. Selecting the components and stuffing the limbs can be done in a preliminary session, assembling the basic puppets in a second. Decorating and completing the final details can be accomplished in a third and final session.

Materials: Two pairs panty hose; newspapers; large detergent or other box; paper plate; four medium sized rubber bands or elastic; 24 inch length of ribbon; construction paper; assorted throw aways such as egg cartons, small boxes, bottle caps, etc.; and yarn, scrap fabric, cotton, buttons and trims.

Construction: Cut each panty hose in half. Stuff each of the four separate legs with crumpled newspaper. Cut a slit in the two upper corners and two lower corners of box top and bottom lids as shown. Tuck end of each stuffed hose into one of the slit corners of box; staple hose to slit lid flap.

Glue paper plate to upper section of box for head. A set of holes close together can be punctured in upper box back to loop ribbon through for tying to neck of child. Staple or sew a rubber band or piece of elastic to end of each limb for securing to child's wrists and ankles. Cardboard hands and feet can also be added to end of limbs. The basic puppet is now complete. Create features and costuming for puppet with scrap fabric, paper, trim, etc. Recycled clothing may also be added to give character.

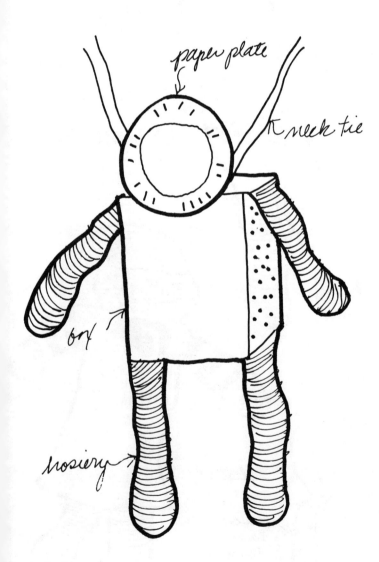

paper plate

neck tie

box

hosiery

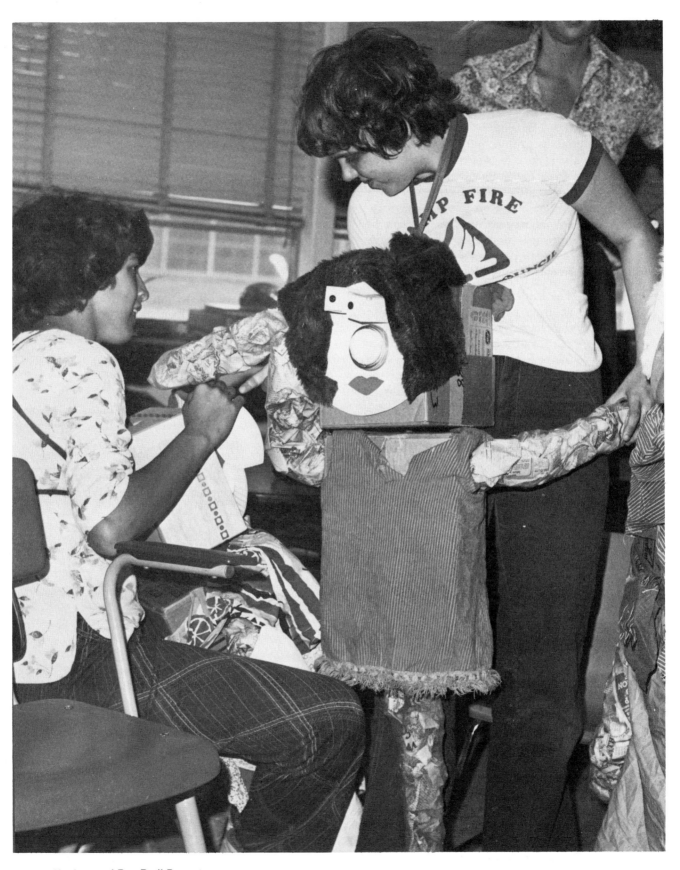

Hosiery and Box Bodi-Puppet

Suggestions for Stories Using Bodi-Puppets

• **The Wind Blew**

The Wind Blew, Pat Hutchins. New York, Mac-Millan Publishing Co., 1974.

A simple story with exciting action centered around the weather, *The Wind Blew* makes challenging story material to explore with children while teaching them about the effects of the elements. The Wind, depicted by a Paper Bag Bodi-Puppet with crepe paper streamers attached, can effectively flow about the space. Other characters in the story, mainly pedestrians, do not require puppets but can be given appropriate props—umbrella, balloon, scarf, etc. The text can easily be changed to suit other available clothing garments or props found in the room.

Approach: The leader narrates the story while children pantomime the actions of the characters. The Wind character can take the props one by one from the pedestrians and place them on a shelf, then return them to the pedestrians at the end of the story.

Puppets/Props: Wind—Paper Bag Bodi-Puppet

Mr. White
Priscilla
Man in hat
Child with kite   *Children*
Housewife with shirt   *with or*
Woman with hanky   *without*
Judge   *puppets*
Postman
Flagpole
Twins
Man with newspaper

Umbrella
Balloon   *Real or*
Hat   *paper cutout*
Kite
Shirt
Hanky
Wig
Letter
Flag
Two Scarves
Newspaper

Preparation: Assign one child to play the Wind with the Bodi-Puppet. Designate a shelf or tabletop where the Wind can place items. Designate another area to be the Sea.

Assign children to play the pedestrian roles and give each character an appropriate prop to hold.

Arrange the children in order of appearance to one side of the playing space. Put the Wind in the center. Suggest actions for the children.

Introduction: Discuss with the children the weather elements—rain, wind, snow, and others. What do they like best about the element wind? What are the good things wind does for us? The bad things?

Story Actions: The Wind blows the _____ (grabs each item and places on shelf)

Umbrella from Mr. White
Balloon from Priscilla
Hat from man
Shirt from housewife
Kite from child
Hanky from woman
Wig from judge
Letter from postman
Flag from pole
Scarves from twins
Newspaper from man

Wind gives items back to everyone then blows out to sea.

Follow-Up Activities: Retell the story using other characters and props the children invented.

paper streamers

The Wind

• **Joseph Had a Little Overcoat**

Joseph Had a Little Overcoat, Simms Taback. New York, Random House, 1977.

This is a marvelous story to teach children vocabulary related to clothing. The action centers around a strong lead character, Joseph, whose tattered old coat is cut down in successive stages from jacket to vest, scarf, necktie and finally a button! Such changes are particularly appropriate for a Bag Bodi-Puppet to which paper costumes can be secured with double-stick tape. Idea by Grace Schmidt, Austin Public Library.

Approach: Leader narrates the story while a child wearing the Joseph Bodi-Puppet and follows the action, changing costume pieces as the story progresses. Or, the entire class could wear Joseph puppets and act as a unit when the story is read.

Puppets/Props: Joseph—Paper Bag Bodi-Puppet

Sister—A child without a puppet

Jacket
Vest

Scarf   *Paper cutouts with*
Tie   *double-stick tape*
Handkerchief   *on backs.*
Button

Chorus—*Several children*

Tea—*Real*

Book—*Real*

Preparation: Assign a child to play Joseph. Another child may be asked to help Joseph change costumes.

Designate one area of the playing space to be the fairgrounds, another area the Sister's home.

Locate the Sister at her home, Joseph in a central space and the chorus to one side. Cue the children on their actions.

Introduction: Let the children share their experiences with recycled clothes. Have they ever had a garment that was cut down or made into another garment? Lead into activity with a statement of this type, "I know a story about someone who had an old coat that became many things."

Story Actions: Joseph—Shows overcoat, replaces it with jacket.
Goes to the fair.

Replaces jacket with vest.
Replaces vest with scarf.
Sings in chorus.
Replaces scarf with tie.
Goes to visit his Sister.
Replaces tie with handkerchief.
Drinks tea.
Replaces handkerchief with button.
Loses button and looks for it.
Writes a book.

Follow-Up Activities: Ask the children to create other paper costumes for Joseph to recycle.

Using Simple Puppets for Story Presentations

The wide selection of puppet construction methods available can enable the storyteller to choose those techniques which are most appropriate to the given situation. For instance, when working with children who have disparate degrees of limitations within a particular handicap, search out those ideas that can challenge the average child in the group. In some cases a restricted time block may necessitate using ready-made puppets. However, since the creation of the puppet itself is therapeutic to a child, whenever possible consider using some of the simple constructions for puppets which are described in the following section. Such techniques allow more time for application and use while creating a balance with puppetmaking activities.

Even a ten minute segment is sufficient to complete quickie puppets such as a picture on a drinking straw or a face drawn on a paper bag. Remember, that an activity that centers around a story becomes more meaningful to the child if he has created the actual characters in the story prior to its telling. It is a way of weaving the child more intimately into the story while establishing a bond between child and story.

If a child is severely limited in her capacities to create features for a puppet, then consider letting the child choose images from magazines and greeting cards such as a picture of a dog or flower. The leader can cut out the shapes for the child to paste onto the basic puppet to suggest character. This is quick and easy and still involves the child in making choices in executing the puppet's final design. An alternate idea is to provide the child with a selection of precut paper circles, triangles and squares that can be glued onto the bag's surface to form features. Ears of varying lengths may be added to this selection. A number of simple puppet construction ideas are given in the following sections.

• Basic Hand Puppet

A basic hand puppet is a traditional puppet form that will find many purposes in the classroom. This puppet features a body that is quite flexible when made from soft material, making it a perfect vehicle for exploring finger and hand exercises, and strengthening muscles. They are flat, easy to store puppets and an entire cast may be collected for continual storytime and classroom activities. A barnyard cast can serve many popular stories and songs, community members such as police officer and mail deliverer are handy for neighborhood study. Holiday characters such as a witch or Santa will become popular additions.

Materials: Giving paper bag paper or fabric such as muslin, old sheet, cotton or medium weight Pellon (interfacing material); felt scraps; and yarn, cotton, buttons and trim.

Construction: Cut out two body pieces from grocery bag paper or fabric following pattern. Line up pieces and glue or staple (paper), or sew (fabric) edges together. (Or, sew pieces right sides together then turn right sides out for a more finished look.) Bottom of puppet should be left open for inserting hand. Coloring medium such as crayons and felt-tip marker pens can be used to color in features and decorate puppets made from muslin, sheet or Pellon. Magazine pictures or photographs of a face can be glued to head area of the puppet. Yarn and cotton make excellent hair. Use felt and other trim for decoration.

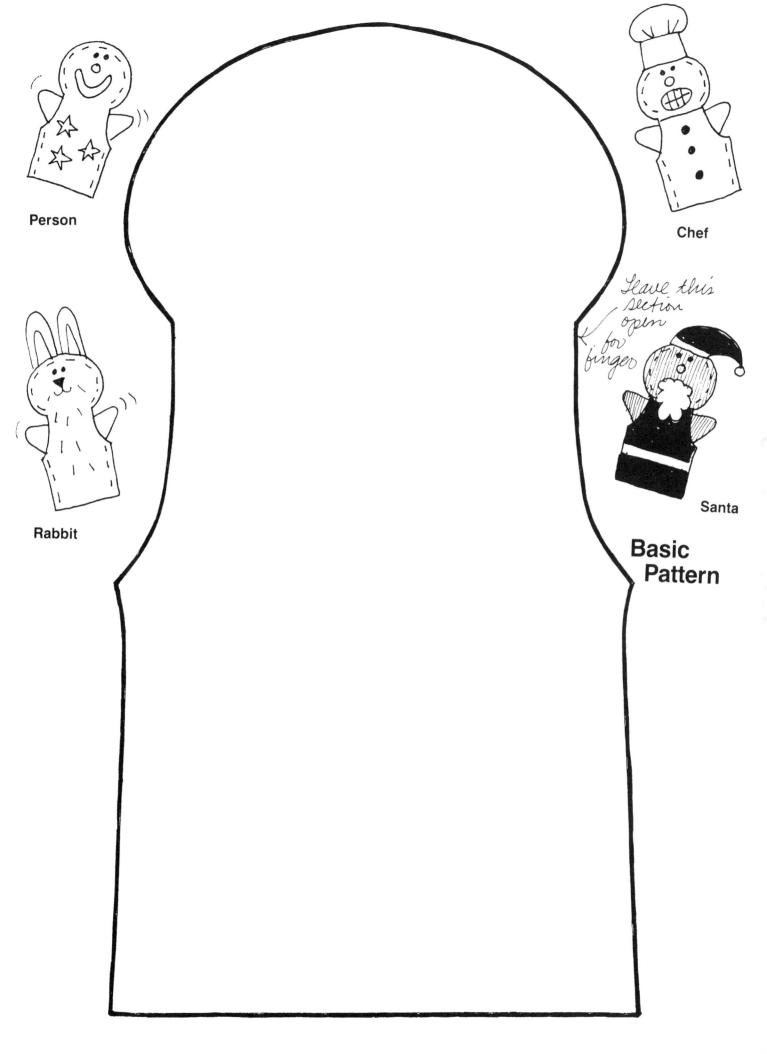

Person

Chef

Rabbit

Leave this
section
open
for
finger

Santa

**Basic
Pattern**

• Stick Puppet

Stick Puppets are the easiest of all the puppet types to construct and can be held by almost any child, even those whose fingers are in a clenched position. The characters can be drawn with crayons or felt-tipped marker pens on paper and taped onto the end of a drinking straw or other rod control. In addition, cutouts from greeting cards and magazine pictures also make excellent sources for casting. Consider using Stick Puppets to portray nonhuman forms in stories. An image of an engine, boat, water waves, or beach ball for example can be taped to a stick control and provided with movements to complement the story's actions. Children delight in seeing an engine chug along, waves undulate up and down or the ball bounce about by means of the stick control.

Materials: Magazine picture, drawing, or photo-copy of pattern; popsicle or ice cream stick, or drinking straw; and crayons or felt-tipped marker pens.

Construction: Cut out and color the picture image and glue or tape it to a stick or straw. These puppets can be called upon to express a number of simple but basic movements such as hopping, walking or dancing from side to side.

• Paper-Bag Puppet

The paper bag has always been one of the most popular materials for puppetmaking. Its sturdy surface gives options for gluing, pasting, spattering and other decorative techniques. Also the flap is a natural for a talking mouth that is easily manipulated by most children and aids in strengthening the fingers and hands.

Materials: Small or medium-size paper bag; construction paper; and scrap fabric and trims.

Construction: Lay bag flat on table. Glue facial features on upper part of bag. Decorate the bottom part with coloring medium or scrap fabric. Add paper arms and legs if desired.

Humpty Dumpty Stick Puppet

paper petals

Flower

Elephant

Doctor

• Envelope Puppet

The natural pointed mouth of this puppet makes a basic form for appealing creatures such as a mouse, chicken or fish. With the addition of a paper nose they can also be cast as people. The standard letter-size envelope is ideal to form the talking mouth, with upper and lower jaw that fits comfortably over a child's small hand. Because the mouth is flexible, it can be used to encourage dialogue or speech. Also, the open/close movements required to operate the mouth are excellent for strengthening finger dexterity through manipulation exercises.

Materials: 6½ x 3½ inch letter envelope; construction paper; and scrap fabric and trims.

Construction: Tuck flap of envelope inside envelope. Place your hand inside envelope, as shown. Gently "bite" fingers of other hand to form the mouth and straighten out any wrinkles. Apply eyes, ears, tongue, and other features with coloring medium or paper cutouts. Add a body by stapling a construction paper or fabric cutout shape to the bottom of head.

• Cup Puppet

Cup Puppets are comfortable puppets to hold, even by a child who has minimal coordination in the hand, because the puppet can be easily slipped over either the opened or closed fist. Just about any lesson can be enlivened with Cup Puppets.

Materials: Paper or styrofoam cup; construction paper; and scrap fabrics, yarn and trims.

Construction: To make a Cup Puppet, add features to cup with coloring medium or paper cutouts. Yarn and fringed paper make excellent hair or whiskers. Place the cup head over the top of the hand. A piece of fabric may be attached around the bottom of the cup to cover the hand if desired.

Robot

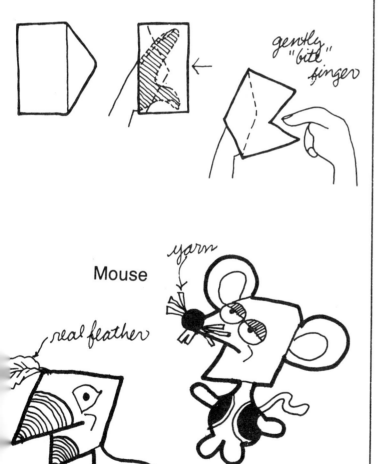

Mouse

Chick

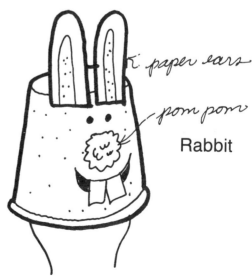

Rabbit

69

• Talking Paper Plate Puppet

A talking Paper Plate Puppet gives superb finger dexterity practice for a child. Small paper plates are recommended for children with small or weak hands as they are easier to hold, large plates for children with normal strength in hands. This puppet has the ability to open its mouth wide making it one of the best types for speech practice. Tongue and teeth can be drawn on the inside of the plates, lips on the outside for speech reference, or, a tongue may be constructed from a strip of felt or paper and glued inside the mouth. Left loose at the end, it can be maneuvered up and down with the other hand to demonstrate the tongue's position when making various sounds. Large paper plates make excellent monster or "Loud Mouth" puppets, characters which delight children.

Materials: Two small or large paper plates; two medium rubber bands; construction paper; and scrap fabrics, yarn and trims.

Construction: Staple a rubber band across the back of each paper plate, about two inches down from top, as shown. Put both paper plates together with rubber band ends facing top and staple plates secure. A paper or fabric body can be attached to the bottom plate.

To Operate: Slip fingers under rubber band on top plate and thumb under rubber band on bottom plate; open and close hand.

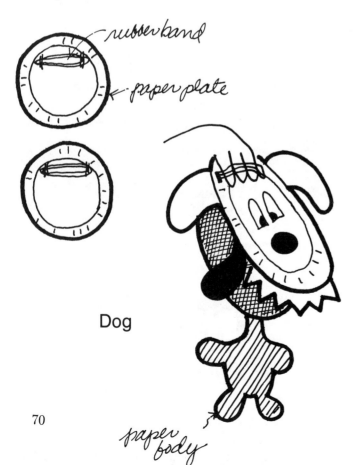

rubber band

paper plate

Dog

paper body

70

• String Puppet

Almost all children are intrigued with the mechanical abilities of string puppets or marionettes. Simplified versions of string puppets can prove valuable in adapting story presentations for children who have handicaps. Deaf children who are keenly animated themselves in expressing body movements and gestures will look to these puppets as models for further awareness. If possible, bring in a commercial string puppet that is capable of achieving interesting movements. Let the children observe the puppet in motion and even mimic the puppet's movements. By waving an arm, raising hands or hopping on one foot the puppet can lead can lead a version of the game "Simon Says." In addition, the children can take turns operating the puppet or performing minor feats with it for the group.

Because the string puppet requires balance to control it, this puppet form is also beneficial for handicapped children who have difficulty in this area. Some multi-handicapped children have to make a special effort to walk or carry a lunch tray steadily. Learning to walk with a string puppet provides motivation for them to acquire improved motor skills along with hand-eye coordination. Practice sessions are more fun if the children can be asked to make their puppets perform simple tasks such as walking to a certain spot, sitting down on the floor or hopping along. Simple versions of string puppets can have one or two hand controls (one for each hand). With two controls, there is opportunity for the children to experiment with up and down motions for achieving balance.

The larger playing spaces necessary to accomodate the string puppets appeal to children who have excessive energies. The hyperactive child has opportunity to focus attention on the finer details of the puppet's movements as he guides the puppet through the spaces. Use as much of the classroom space as possible, enlarging the territory where the story's actions are dramatized. Some simple scenic props, strategically located around the space, will give the children gravitational points. A pond can be represented by a circle of blue paper, a house made from a grocery carton, or real toys can serve as vehicles. A sheet of mural paper stretched between two chairs, spaced apart, makes an excellent backdrop for painted scenery.

These puppets also are compatible with many stories. The popular long-legged bird made from styrofoam balls found in many craft or toy shops would fit in perfectly with a story such as *What Lilly Goose Found* by Annabelle Sumera.

The ideas in this section for constructing string puppets are simple ones using one to three strings.

Puppets with more than three strings are usually complex and should be saved for advanced projects only. The building materials for this type of puppet are open to invention: balloons, boxes, rolled-up newspaper, and magazine pictures with pleated legs are among the things which can be used for the basic body. The following section describes several methods for constructing String Puppets ranging from easy to more advanced techniques.

• Instant String Puppets

Instant String Puppets can be made from drawings or pictures cut from magazines and greeting cards. The pictures should be large enough to define the character clearly. The addition of pleated paper legs and arms will give the puppet bouncy limbs for active participation. In this case partially cut out pictures may be used. For example, the legs can be omitted from a magazine picture of a tiger and the pleated legs substituted.

Materials: Magazine picture, greeting card or drawing; string; 1 ½ inch wide strips of construction paper; and cardboard towel tube.

Construction: Cut out picture and add pleated legs and/or arms. Attach one or two strings to top of puppet and secure to a tube hand control.

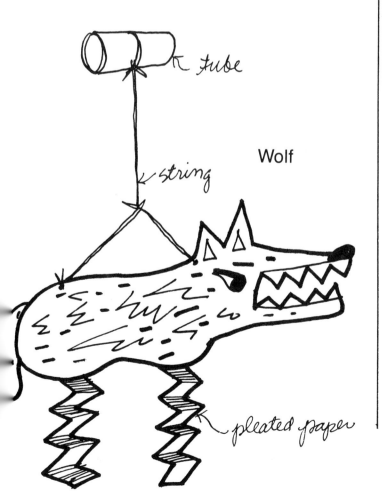

Wolf

• Newspaper String Puppet

The construction of Newspaper String Puppets provides motor activity that aids in strengthening fingers, especially in the process of crumpling and rolling the newspaper. This spontaneous puppet building project can be left with the exposed newspaper, or paint and decorations can be added. The main components of this type puppet are crumpled balls and rolled tubes of newspaper secured with masking tape. These building blocks are excellent for creating numerous interesting combinations and characters.

Materials: Newspaper; masking tape; string; cardboard tubes; and scrap fabrics, yarn and trims.

Construction: *To make paper balls*—open out the newspaper and crumple it up into a wad. Increase the size of the ball by adding newspaper to the circumference of the initial ball. Wrap strips of masking tape entirely around the ball to secure newspaper.

To make rolled tubes—keep newspaper folded and lay flat on table or floor; starting at one end roll up into tight tube. Wrap tape around the tube in several places.

To assemble—make various size balls and tubes and link together with string, masking tape or stapler. Lengths of string can be taped to the parts and secured to cardboard tube controls.

To decorate—colored felt-tipped marker pens can be used to create instant features. Use paint, paper or scrap fabrics for additional decorations. Experiment with fringed newspaper for hair, feathers and fur effects. The addition of a pleated section of newspaper will make a fine turkey tail, wings or elephant ears.

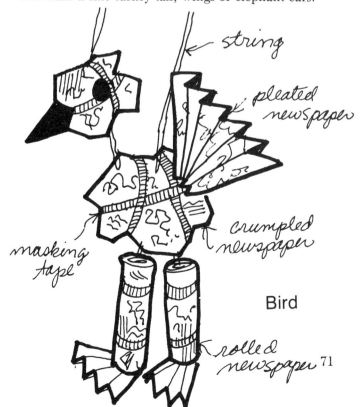

Bird

71

• Wrist Puppet

For children who have very limited motor abilities in the arms, wrist puppets are excellent companions. Two types of wrist puppets may be explored—Bracelet Puppets and Box Wrist Puppets. Although all young children enjoy wearing them, Puppet Bracelets are particularly designed for physically impaired children who might otherwise not be able to manipulate a puppet. These decorative bracelets are playful images of paper or felt puppet characters attached to ribbons. When worn on the wrist, the Bracelets present a strong visual focus to encourage motor control and motivate physically handicapped children to perform repetitive motor exercises and stimulate hand/eye coordination. A flower, monkey, bird or other image is suitable for these simple characters. A search through magazines will uncover some quick imagery for cutting out and attaching to ribbons and integrating into stories, songs or other activities. A large, brightly colored letter or number can also be worn to emphasis beginning sounds or vowels.

A box also serves well as a base for a puppet to be worn on the wrist and presents a three dimensional from for the child to operate. A pudding, cosmetic or other small box should be used. The Box Puppet is secured to the child's wrist and hangs down as the child explores such movements as hopping, walking, swinging by means of a rubber band and dancing with the dangling puppet making it ideally suited for rabbit, dancing clown and other lively character. An alternate method of operation is to fit the rubber band so that it is barely snug on the child's wrist, with the box character sitting on *top* of the wrist, rather than hanging down. This perching position is particularly appropriate for a snail or turtle puppet. In either case, if the child does not wish to wear the puppet, this particular puppet can be simply held by the rubber band with the finger and bounced up and down.

Puppet Bracelet

Materials: Magazine picture, photograph and/or drawing or felt cutout of character; 1 inch wide ribbon (approximately 10 inches long); scraps of paper and fabric; and velcro (optional).

Construction: Cut out each character from paper or felt and staple it onto a strip of ribbon. Add features and decorate with scraps of paper or material where appropriate. Feathers, yarn and cotton puffs add nice additional touch experiences to puppets. Tie the ribbon in a bow around the child's wrist or if desired secure it with a piece of velcro which has been sewn onto the ribbon.

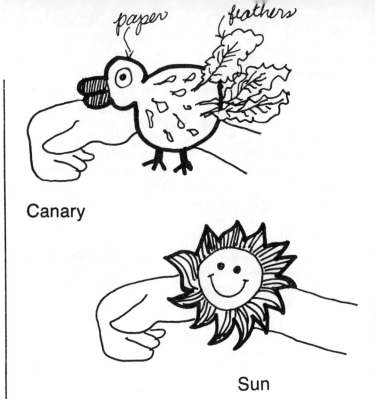

Canary

Sun

Box Wrist Puppet

Materials: Pudding, toothpaste, cosmetic or other small box; large rubber band; construction paper; and yarn, buttons and trim.

Construction: Staple the rubber band to the top of the box prior to taping the box's lid down; add paper features and decorate. Pleated paper strips make bouncy limbs. Add yarn or cotton hair.

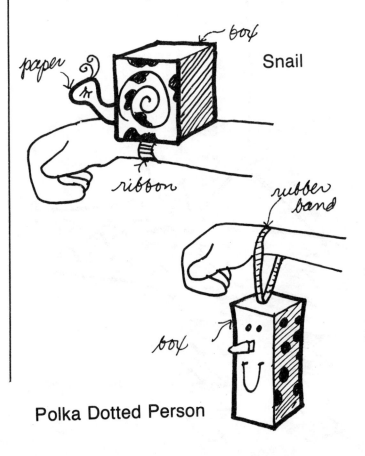

Snail

Polka Dotted Person

• Foot Puppet

For children who have minimal motor dexterity in the feet, Foot Puppets can bring new enjoyment and motivation to excercises and other activities. Animal characters can be asked to join in with general thereapy and participate in aiding the child strengthen feet and leg muscles or they can serve as a focus for teaching curriculum or involve the child in storytime as would other puppet types. The child could be positioned comfortably on the floor or in a bed when operating the puppets. It has to be decided whether the puppet should face the child (for individual activities,) or an audience (in the event of a performance for friends or family.) The puppet can be adjusted to the proper view. By adding a face and features, slippers and socks make the sturdiest puppets for foot wear. Search about for some appealing soft fluffy type slippers and colorful socks to add to cast. If the child is adept she may want to play two characters, one on each foot. The addition of felt ears, pom pom noses and other features to the basic slipper or sock puppet makes a simple assembly. Advanced students may enjoy creating amore detailed construction. Also available in many stores are ready made animal slipper characters.

Materials: Slipper or sock; round or square sponge; felt scraps; and yarn, cotton and trim.

Construction: Split sponge up the middle half way. Spread split ends apart and slip sponge over toe of slipper or sock to serve as head. Secure by hand sewing in several places or rubber cementing in place. Felt features and yarn or cotton hair can be added to head with rubber cement. Add felt arms to sock and decorate to suit the character.

Sad/Glad People

• Bodi-Costumes and Masks

Although costumes and masks do not fall in the same category as puppets, they share with them similar attributes, especially in the extended use of creative dramatics. Children with handicaps particularly enjoy role playing and the special attention given them in donning a costume when acting out parts. There is a certain dazzle to a child who has just become a fairy or princess in a tinfoil crown or a ladybug with spotted, flapping wings. Through Bodi-Costumes, as with the Bodi-Puppet in previous parts of this book, the child becomes at one with the character and intimately enmeshed into the story's actions and dialogue. Playacting animate as well as inanimate forms such as trees, flowers, grass or even ocean waves with the addition of simple costume suggestions can be fascinating. Simple tree foliage or flower petals cut from paper can surround a child's face, or blue paper streamers to represent water can be attached to the body to enhance the basic idea. Asking questions, "How does a tree stand? A flower grow? Or, waves roll in a storm?" will aid the child in dramatizing specific roles. Bodi-Costumes are suited to many storybooks but are particularly interesting when animals, monsters or other nonhuman characters are cast, so that the costume more clearly distinguishes from the basic human form. Famous people in history, inventors, explorers and holiday characters are also colorful to characterize through costuming and the related events become memorable when dramatized. Science is another subject matter which offers a wealth of material for interpreting with Bodi-Costumes. Children can portray planets by wearing large circular shapes on the front of their bodies and act out the relationships and movement

Paper Flower Masks

patterns. The habitats of fish, dinosaurs, wildlife, birds or insects could be depicted through costumes. As an example, creation of a simple paper costume for a ladybug could convey information: "Are their eyes black? Do they have two sets of wings? What does a ladybug eat? Are they aphids?"

Let the costume be as simple as possible. It is not necessary to invest time and energy in making elaborate examples. Mere suggestion is all that is required to define the character as the children's imaginations will fill in the rest. Paper ears on headbands for a rabbit or dog, a beard and red hat for Santa Claus, and tophat for Abe Lincoln, antennas for an outer space creature and paper wings for a bird or butterfly will all serve well in developing a cast. Costumes that are too fussy will only be awkward to cope with and interfere with the presentation.

Utilize the classroom's spaces and furnishings to improvise settings or props for the stories dramatized with Bodi-Costumes. The space under a table can represent a house or beehive, a small rug a pond, or a chair a vehicle. The room itself can be divided into specific locales where the action occurs. In "Little Red Riding Hood," for example, one side of the room could be designated as her home, the center area the woods, and the opposite side Granny's house. If one of the puppeteers is in a wheelchair, consider integrating it into the story as a key prop such as a boat or throne.

Basic Puppet Features

The following pages of features can be photocopied for classroom use and help simplify puppet-making activities for the teacher, especially in cases where children have limited motor dexterity. The children can select features of their choosing and color them in with crayons or marker pens. Coloring within lines is an extremely beneficial exercise for aiding in hand/eye coordination. The features can then be glued onto a paper bag, plate, cup, box, or other materials used for puppets.

Paper Bag Puppet with cut out features

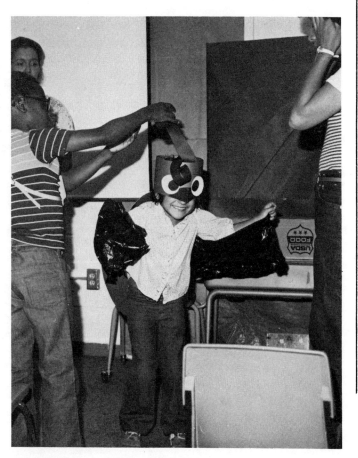

Paper and Plastic LadyBug Bodi-Costume

Feature pages are printed with courtesy of **Puppetry and Early Childhood Education** — by Tamara Hunt and Nancy Renfro

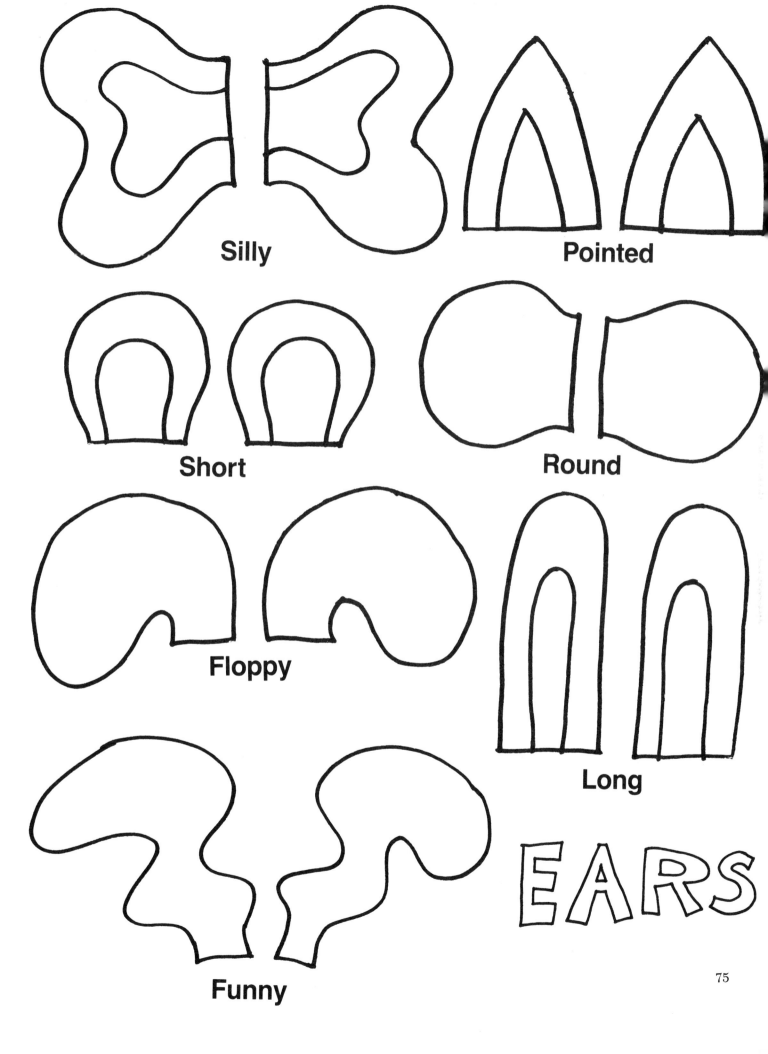

Silly

Pointed

Short

Round

Floppy

Long

Funny

EARS

75

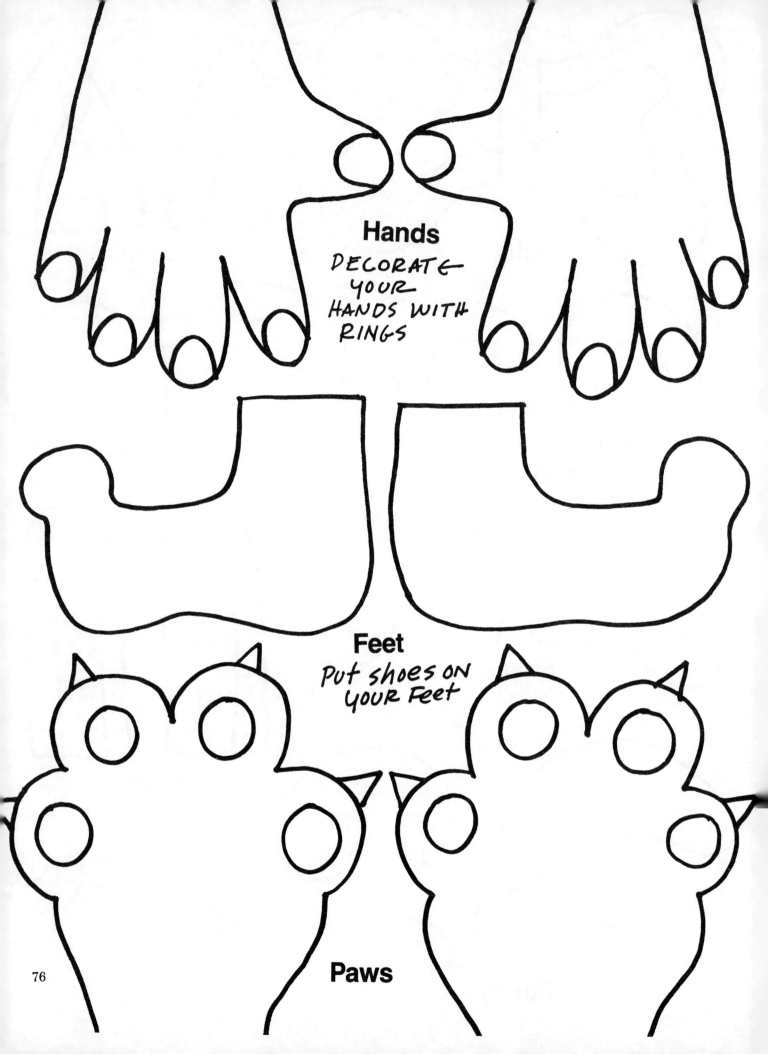

Hands

DECORATE
YOUR
HANDS WITH
RINGS

Feet

PUT SHOES ON
YOUR FEET

Paws

76

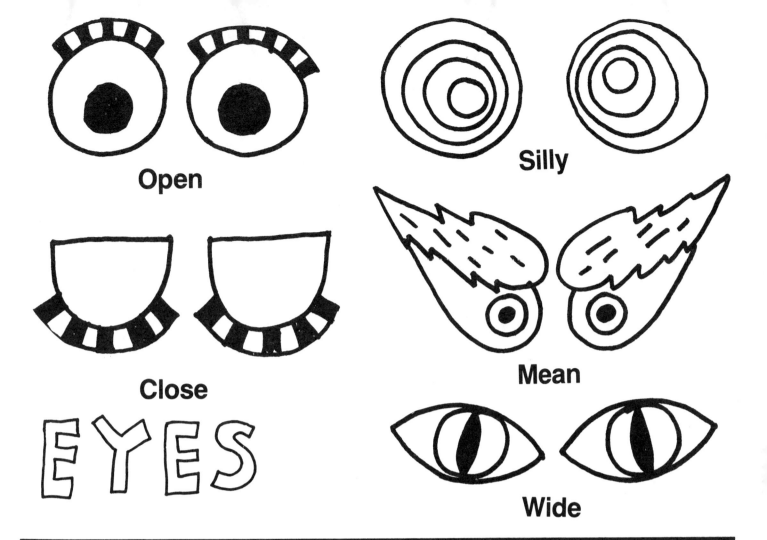

Open

Silly

Mean

Close

EYES

Wide

Pretty

Happy

Sad

Mean

Silly

MOUTHS

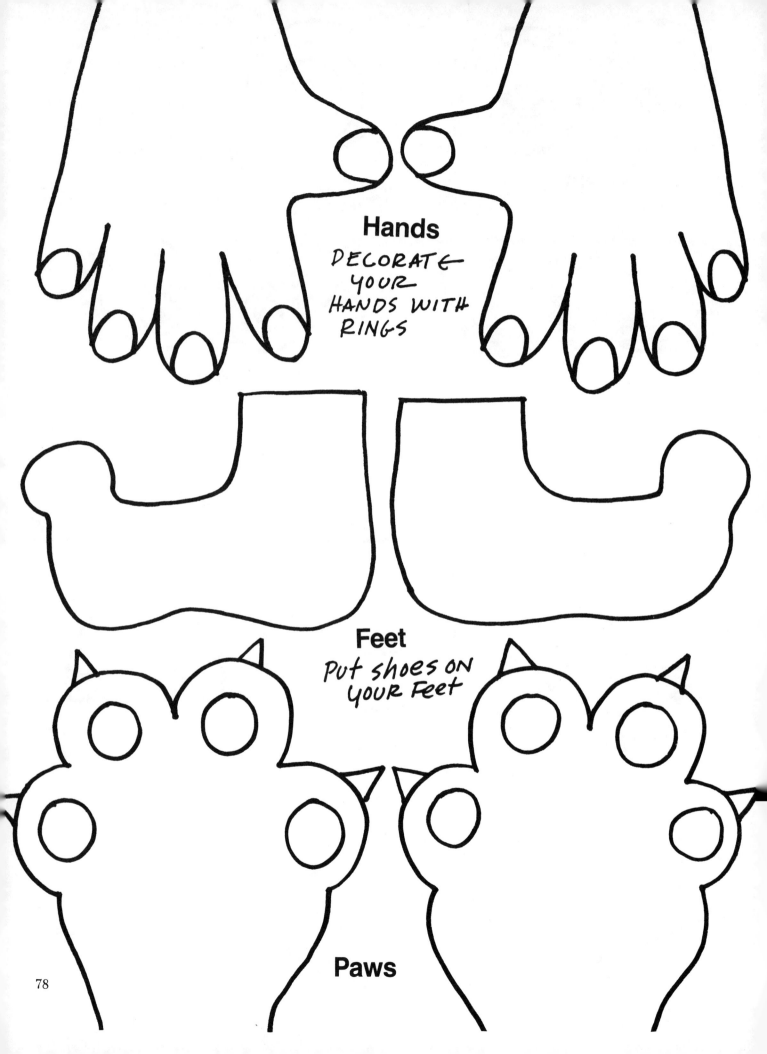

Hands

DECORATE YOUR HANDS WITH RINGS

Feet

Put shoes on your feet

Paws

Books on the Arts

Art Activities for the Handicapped. Sally M. Atack. Prentice Hall. New York, 1982. A well written book about art and its value to the disabled. Discovery and exploration of self, art as a language, physical dexterity along with directed activities are included.

Arts and Crafts for the Physically and Mentally Disabled. Elaine and Loren Gould. Charles C. Thomas. Springfield IL, 1978. Special focus on activities for those children with physical or mental handicaps.

Art in the Elementary School. Marlene M. Linderman. Wm. C Brown Publishers. Dubuque, IA, 1979. A lovely and beautifully presented book on art and art appreciation with emphasis on building perceptual and other type awarenesses.

Art for Exceptional Children. Donald M. Uhlin. Wm. C. Brown Co. Dubuque, IA, 1979. A comprehensive craft and art book for helping the handicapped child structure and maintain a reality. Concludes with interesting section on brain functioning and creativity.

It's Me! Building Self Concepts Through Art. June H. Campbell. Teaching Resources. New York, 1977. A superb book with an extensive collection of craft and art ideas based on the theme of building better self-concepts.

Bibliography

Airport. Byron Barton. Harper and Row, 1982. New York.
This clearly graphic book illustrates the working mechanics of a typical airport.

Buzz, Buzz, Buzz. Byron Barton. Penguin Books, Inc. 1979 New York.
A bee who stings a bull causes a chain reaction and havoc on a peaceful farm.

Joseph Had a Little Overcoat. Simms Taback. Random House, 1977. New York.
Conservation is the theme for this story about a man's coat that is cut down in various recycling stages.

Looking for Suzie. Bernadine Cook—illus. by Judith Shahn. Addison-Wesley, 1959. Reading, MA.
Children on a farm go in search for Suzie, their pet cat, among the territory of the farm. They discover her in the hayloft with her new born kittens.

Octavius. Betty Hubka. Steck Vaughn, 1963. Austin, TX.
A delightful story about an octopus who changes colors to express emotions.

The Wind Blew. Pat Hutchins. Macmillan Books, 1974. New York.
The wind creates a great deal of action as it sweeps through a town, carrying away innumerous items only to be returned to the people afterwards.

Voyage of Jim. Janet Barber, illus. by Fritz Wagner. Carol Rhoda Books, 1973. Minneapolis, MN.
Jim, a mouse, goes on a fantastic sea voyage and meets various creatures on the islands along the way.

What Lilly Goose Found. Annabelle Sumera. Western Publishing Inc. 1979. Racine, WI.
Lilly Goose goes on a walk and encounters a series of silly incidents evolving around every day objects that she finds and misconstrues for other things.

ENHANCING SPEECH ACTIVITIES THROUGH PUPPETRY

By Nancy Renfro

A special acknowledgment is made to *Debbie Sullivan* and to speech therapists *Bonnie Orr* and *Trenna Pickett* for consultation and inspiration in compiling the ideas in this chapter.

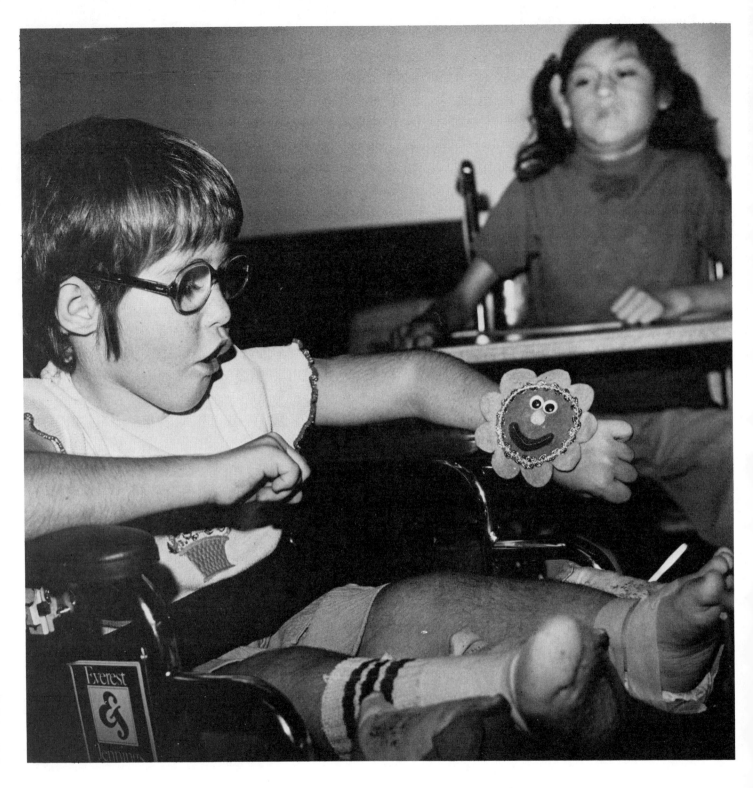

Puppets provide strong visual reinforcement of concepts—*Bracelet Puppet*

Enhancing Speech Activities Through Puppetry

By Nancy Renfro

Speech activities are an integral part of the language arts program and the handicapped child can profit from extensive exposure to speech exercises. Unfortunately, these processes often involve repetitive drills which are boring and do not challenge the child. Puppetry can offer innovative techniques which command attention and help children overcome self-consciousness. Aided by a puppet, the teacher is able to focus on speech problems without subjecting the child to the embarrassment of repeated corrections.

Whether speech disability is caused by a hearing impairment, a physical impediment or an emotional block, the affected child is often set apart from peer groups. Society tends to equate intelligence with proper speech so that even a minor speech distortion can establish psychological barriers which further handicap the child. Consequently, it is important to provide a nonthreatening atmosphere which will motivate the child to change or improve speech patterns. Puppetry is an excellent vehicle for this situation. The following suggestions highlight some of the general ways in which puppets may be used in the speech program or classrooms.

• Puppets provide strong visual reinforcement of concepts and help children assimilate the basic sound of language. For instance, a friendly snake is excellent for exploring those s sounds!

• Puppets are superb for carrying children through the actual production of language via conversations, skits and dramatizations.

• Existing textbook materials may be adapted to include puppets. If a lesson requires that specific words or sounds be repeated, the child may be asked to select a puppet to mimic them. In this way, the focus is taken away from the child and placed on the puppet instead. Any mistakes made during the drill are attributed to the puppet rather than the child.

• A puppet may be used as a "third person" for such activities as interrogative reversal. A teacher holding a monkey character could ask the child, "Is this a monkey?" whereas the child would respond, "Yes, he is a monkey."

• The addition of a tongue to a puppet is beneficial in many cases. For example, when a tongue depressor and/or flashlight is required to study a child's throat for an oral peripheral test, the procedure may be demonstrated on the puppet first to show the child there is nothing to fear.

• Headphones placed on a puppet will also help the child to feel more at ease with such standard procedures.

• Puppets can demonstrate how to use objects in the classroom as well as everyday items such as a spoon or a comb as a means of exploring conversation.

• A puppet may be used as a control device to direct attention and quieten the class. For example, Woofer, a dog puppet, could have extra long ears. When the class beocmes too noisy, the teacher could cover Woofer's eyes with his ears as a signal for the class to quieten down.

• Child-made puppets give marvelous opportunities for exploring descriptive language. Various textures glued to large supermarket bags make excellent puppets for such activities.

For the teacher choosing to integrate puppetry into a program, the exercises and activities in this chapter suggest a number of ways in which puppets can be used in the language arts program to improve speech skills, develop vocabulary and facilitate oral practice. Since the creative process fosters pride and self-esteem, the teacher is encouraged to allow children to make the puppets when time constraints and the abilities of the group allow. In addition, many teachers will choose to use these concepts as a basis for developing other ideas appropriate to the needs of the special child who is discovering speech and widening horizons.

• **Fe-Fi-Fo-Fum**

Puppet Type: Wide Mouth Paper-Plate Puppet/ Giant

Objective: To stimulate articulation of initial consonants.

To practice rhyming skills.

Activity: Read the original or a condensed version of the folk tale *Jack and the Beanstalk*.

Have children create a Giant puppet based on the wide-mouth paper-plate construction.

Retell the folktale or excerpts from the tale while emphasizing, for ear training, the "Fe-Fi-Fo-Fum" sounds. Children can be asked to join the chant with their puppets, exaggerating the sounds.

Expand this exercise by substituting other initial consonants "He-Hi-Ho-Hum" or, "Se-Si-So-Sum." (The movable tongue on this puppet can be manually positioned to demonstrate teeth and tongue relationship when pronouncing sounds.)

Suggest that the children, with their puppet's help, search the room for objects with the same initial consonant such as furniture, fan, fork. If objects are sparse for a particular letter, then make up a series of flash cards with magazine pictures or drawings pasted on them for a wider range of words. After practicing with individual sounds, mix cards that include various beginning sounds and let children take turns finding correct words for their Giant puppet to gobble.

To Make Puppet

Materials: Two paper plates; two medium rubber bands; construction paper; yarn or cotton; and scrap fabric and trim.

Construction: Staple a rubber band across the back of each paper plate, about two inches down from top, as shown. Put both paper plates together with rubber band ends facing top and staple plates secure. Children can create paper features for the

Giant and glue onto the plates. Add a large paper or felt tongue to inside mouth and large paper teeth to rim of plates. Fringed paper, yarn or cotton can be used for hair. A paper or fabric body can be attached to the bottom plate. To operate mouth, slip fingers under rubber band on top plate and thumb under rubber band on bottom plate; open and close hand.

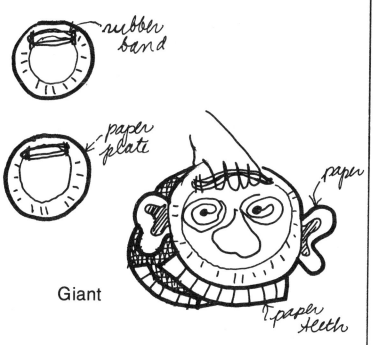

Giant

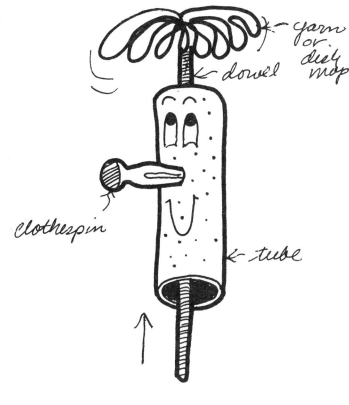

Pop-Up Person

• **Pop-Up Tube Puppets**

Objective: Learn to sustain phonation

Activity: The Pop-Up Puppet can be used to help a child gauge the correct length of breath required to sustain a sound (such as vowels). Let the child begin the sound with the puppet's hair in the low position. As the sound lengthens raise the hair accordingly. Continue to raise until the proper breath length is achieved.

To Make Puppet

Materials: Cardboard towel tube; clothespin; construction paper; yarn; and dowel.

Construction: Paint a face on the cardboard tube. Or, tube can be covered completely with colored paper for a smoother look. Puncture a hole and insert clothespin through hole for nose. Glue in place. Create a small mop of hair by bunching together some yarn, tying it in the middle and attaching it to the end of dowel. Insert other end of dowel through tube. Pop dowel up and down.

• **Ghostly Sounds**

Puppet Type: Revolving Paper-Plate Puppet/Ghost

Objectives: To differentiate vowel sounds.

Activity: The Revolving Ghost Puppet serves as a model for this lesson. Explain to the children that ghosts make a wide range of sounds.

Turn the plate disc on the Ghost Puppet to show a particular vowel. As the vowel appears in the puppet's mouth, ask the children to mimic the proper sound along with the Ghost.

Make a series of small paper ghost cutouts and write a word on the back of each one to match the vowels. Ask children to find words to match vowels that correspond to those in the puppet's mouth.

Ask each child to recite an action for the Ghost to follow based on a word using a vowel just studied. For example:

85

Gate—The ghost opens and shuts the gate.

Cat—The ghost chases a cat around the room.

Hold—The ghost holds the book.

To Make Puppet

Materials: Two paper plates; paper fastener; and white construction paper or paper toweling.

Construction: Cut a 2-inch diameter hole in lower section of one plate. Lay a second plate behind the first plate and line them up. Locate exact center of plates and punch out a small hole through holes in center of both plates; insert paper fastener through holes in plates. Revolve back plate and draw images on each clear space that appears through the 2-inch mouth hole of the front plate.

Color simple ghost features on plate. Add a white length of paper or towel tissue to bottom of plate for body.

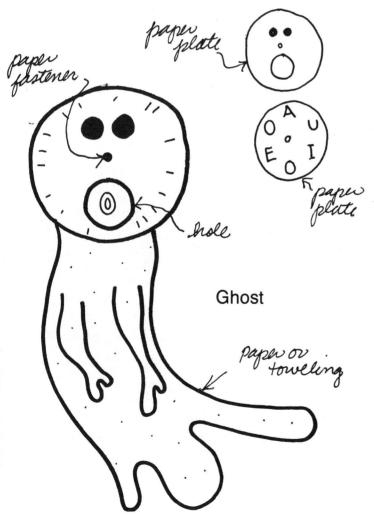

Ghost

- **Fox-in-a-Box**

Puppet Type: Stick Puppet/Fox-in-a-Box

Objective: To understand prepositions.
To learn concept of sequential action.

Activity: Have each child create a Stick Fox Puppet and its box home. If time does not permit puppetmaking, then the leader can make a Fox-in-a-Box model to demonstrate the lesson.

Using the Fox-in-a-Box, let the Fox demonstrate to the children all the things it can do with its box home. Emphasize these and other prepositions.

on	off	around
through	over	across
beside	inside	in front of
	in back of	

Recite a short sequence of events based on the above prepositions; then let the children follow events with their puppets.

For example: The fox was sleeping *inside* the box. The fox woke up and stuck its head *outside* the box. The fox saw a rabbit and chased it *around* the box.

Ask the children to make up their own short skits to present to the group with their puppets based on prepositions.

To Make Puppet

Materials: Pudding or other small box; drinking straw or blunt skewer; and construction paper.

Construction: Cut out and color a fox's head from paper; attach to end of drinking straw or skewer. Cut off top of box. Or, if box has an open and close type lid, open out lid and retain lid. Puncture a hole in bottom of box and insert other end of straw or skewer through hole, hiding fox inside box ready for use.

paper head

Fox

← drinking straw or blunt skewer

- **The Silliest Person in the World**

Puppet Type Cup Puppet/Silliest Person in the World.

Objective: To improve descriptive language.
To become familiar with verbs, adjectives and adverbs.
To learn logical order.

Activity: Ask each child to think of the Silliest Person in the World and create a Cup Puppet character of this person. Encourage exaggeration by giving the character some unusual features (oversized nose, pointed ears, lots of freckles, overly long hair, polka dotted shoes).

Have each child take a turn holding up her completed puppet and describing the character to the group using colorful adjectives. For example, the child might say, "This is the silliest person in the world because he has *purple* hair, *square freckles* and *floppy* ears." For extra reinforcement, you might wish to write down the adjectives for each child's puppet on a piece of paper and pin it to the puppet.

To introduce action verbs to the children, prepare flash cards with various action verbs written on them. Have each child select a card and make up a short action skit to perform for the group with the puppet. Be sure to have the child emphasize the selected type of movement.

Run   Glide   Wave   Walk
Skip   Jump   March   Dance

Next have the class describe the skits orally, using adverbs to clarify the action.

The puppet runs *fast*; the puppet runs *slowly*.

The puppet waves *happily*; the puppet waves *sadly*.

The puppet marches *briskly*; the puppet marches *quietly*.

Write a series of short sentences to make a short story, one sentence per strip of paper. Mix them out of logical order and ask each child to take a turn at unscrambling them and acting out the story with her Silly Person Puppet.

For example:

The silly person took a brisk walk.

He spent the $100 bill on candy and cake and green shoe strings.

The silly person looked down and saw a $100 bill.

or (for two pupppeteers):

The silly persons both went home.

The silly person strolled until he met another silly person.

The two silly persons shook hands.

To Make Puppet

Materials: Paper or styrofoam cup; construction paper; scrap fabric; and buttons, yarn, cotton and trims.

Construction: Turn cup upside down and place over hand. Create silly features from paper to add to the cup. Attach a colorful costume made from scrap fabric to rim of cup. Odds and ends can be used for other decoration.

Silly Person

- Cleo Clown

Puppet Type: Paper Bag Swallowing Puppet/Cleo Clown

Objective: To learn to classify words.

Activity: Use a Swallowing Clown Puppet to lead this exercise. In addition to the puppet, create several groups of small flash cards with pictures from various classification groups pasted or drawn on them for the puppet to swallow. Such groups may include the farm, foods, pets and sealife.

Mix up the cards right side up on a table top; then focus on one classification group at a time. Let each child take a turn picking up a card that matches a specific group. After reciting the word depicted on the card, the child can feed it to Cleo Clown.

The song "I Know a Cleo Clown" can accompany the activity and be sung to the words, "I Know an Old Lady." Substitute the words from the cards. For example:

> I Know a Cleo Clown who swallowed an (Octopus)
> I don't know why he swallowed an (Octopus),
> Perhaps he'll die.

To Make Puppet

Materials: Two supermarket bags; stiff paper or poster board; construction paper; clear acetate (book report cover); and scrap fabric.

Construction: Prepare outer bag—Cut a rectangle window hole in stomach area. Tape a piece of acetate to back of window hole. Cut out a mouth hole as shown. Cut a slit on either side of bag, close to window hole cards and large enough for hand to pull out cardboard.

Slip outer bag over inner bag (which has no cutouts or preparation). Fit together so bags match up perfectly. Staple together bags around entire bottom edge.

Cut a face shape (larger than flap of bag) from paper or poster board and add paper features. Yarn or cotton serves well for hair.

Glue a piece of fabric on front of outer bag for a gay costume. Use trim to decorate. Add poster board arms and legs. Perhaps a funny hat, too!

Cleo Clown

• Opposite Characters

Puppet Type: Paper-Plate Turn Around Puppet/ Opposite Characters

Objective: To become familiar with antonyms. To provide practice in oral expression.

Activity: Ask each child to create a Turn-Around Puppet character that depicts opposite words on each side of the puppet. For example: sad/happy, mean/nice, rich/poor, old/young.

Have each child take a turn describing his puppet's characteristics and what special features make each character different. A sad puppet might have limp hair while a happy puppet bouncy hair. A young puppet smooth skin while an old puppet wrinkled skin.

Ask each child to make up a short skit to present to the group about his opposite characters. For example, a happy person could try to cheer up a sad person or an old person could talk about what she did when she was a young person.

To Make Puppet

Materials: Two paper plates; cardboard towel tube; construction paper; and scrap yarn or cotton.

Construction: Line up the two paper plates and staple the edges together leaving the bottom free for inserting cardboard tube. Slip tube up between the plates and glue in place. With coloring medium and paper create features for each plate. Yarn and cotton can be used for hair. To hold puppet grasp the tube by the hand.

Young/Old

• Nursery Rhymes

Puppet Type: Cup Theater/Nursery Rhymes

Objective: To practice oral expression.

Activity: Ask each child to create a Cup Theater of a nursery rhyme. Nursery rhymes can be written out on flash cards and distributed to the children or they may wish to make their own selections.

When Cup Theaters are completed ask each child to present her rhyme to the group.

To Make Puppet

Materials: Paper or styrofoam cup; drinking straws; and construction paper.

Construction: Cut out and color characters from paper. Attach each character to the end of a drinking straw. Puncture holes in the bottom of the cup and insert other end of each straw through a hole. Paper scenic suggestions such as a flower garden, moon or brick wall can be attached to rim or outer surface of cup.

Jack Be Nimble

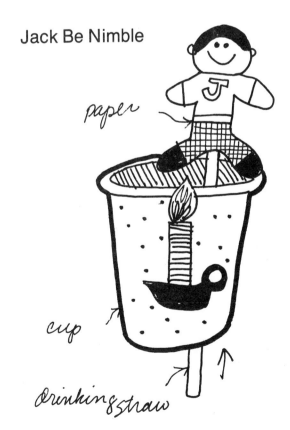

• Talking Tiger

Puppet Type: Box Puppet/Talking Tiger

Objective: To practice reading aloud.

Activity: Use a Tiger Puppet as a model in directing this lesson.

Write a series of simple sentences on a continuous paper strip. Sentences may feature items of special study such as verbs, adjectives, initial consonants and vowels.

Slip sentence strip through the puppet's mouth so the words appear in Talking Tiger's mouth. Ask a child to read the sentence as you move it along. Or, the child may wish to operate the strip herself.

Talking Tiger can be used in other ways. Questions can be written on the strips for a child to respond to, or incomplete sentences can be prepared for the child to fill in.

To Make Puppet

Materials: Detergent or cereal box; 1½ to 2 inch strips of paper; and construction paper.

Construction: Locate the mouth area on the front of box. Cut two vertical slits 3 to 4 inches apart and the height of the paper strip. Also cut a slit at both sides of the box. After you have written words or sentences on the paper strip, thread the strip through the four slits as shown in diagram. Decorate the box with paint and paper features to look like a Tiger.

Talking Tiger

Books on Speech and Language

Clouds; Footsteps; Raindrops; Sunshine; Whispers; and Snowflakes. Don Barnes, Arlene Burgdorf and L. Stanley Wenck. Steck-Vaughn Co. Austin TX, 1975. Activity books include reading, thinking and reasoning skills. Varied activities covering classifying, discriminating between real and fanciful, identifying relationships among events, ordering objects and many more skills.

Going Bananas Over Language Skills. Charlie and Becky Daniel. Good Apple Inc. Carthage IL, 1978. A fun-filled activity book that's good for reinforcing a variety of language activities in areas of punctuation, capitalization and synonyms, antonyms and homonyms.

Kids 'N Katalogs. Louise and M.C. Weber. Incentive Publications, Inc. Nashville TN, 1976. Presents activities and ideas for developing and reinforcing reading skills. The learning experiences are designed to develop skills in word recognition, word meaning, word analysis, comprehension and communication.

Match; Challenge; Feedback; and Spark—Series of books by Scholastics Skills Book. New York, 1974. Activity books which help build reading skills. Practice finding the main idea, picking out important details, sequencing and improving vocabulary. Subjects—how animals survive in the desert, the Pony Express, famous wonders, Sweet James (songwriter), a subway runaway.

P's and Q's for the Sounds We Use. The Kids' Stuff Phonics Book. Imogene Forte and Mary Ann Pangle. Incentive Publications, Inc. Nashville TN, 1978. Fun activities designed to integrate the use of basic comprehension and work attack skills for widely varying levels of phonetic abilities. Stresses individualized settings for diagnostic/prescriptive teaching of phonetic skills.

Phonics File. Bill Eral. Dale Seymour Publications. 1982. Collection of handi-art for creative teachers to choose from, copy and use in their specific language activities.

Secrets and Surprises. Joe Wayman and Lorraine Plum. Good Apple, Inc. Carthage IL, 1977. Dozens of activities and experiences in language arts. Writing, speaking, listening, moving and imagining. Provides structure and stimulus for children's personal creations to evolve into a richer and more fluent language.

Starting Off with Phonics. Virginia Polish. Cross Studio. Modern Curriculum Press. Cleveland OH, 1980. Series of workbooks for language arts and reading programs: Auditory, Visual and Motor Skills; The Alphabet; Consonant Sounds; More Consonant Sounds; Short Vowels; and Long Vowels.

Words Around the Neighborhood. Richard A. Boning. Picto Cabulary Series. Barnell Loft, L.T.D. 958 Church St., Baldwin NY 11510, 1976. Create and stimulate interest in the children's immediate environment and supplement and enrich basic knowledge and vocabulary.

Words Theatre. Richard A. Boning. Barnell Loft, L.T.D. 958 Church St., Baldwin NY 11510, 1979. Promotes active participation of all pupils in multidimensional language experiences. Good for grades 3-6. Each book (there are 4 for each grade level) contains 15 units with 20 work skits per unit.

A MULTIMEDIA APPROACH TO LANGUAGE
By Judith Schwab

Judith Schwab, a professional artist and creative arts consultant from Wilmington, Delaware, with a B.A. from Kean College of New Jersey, has puppeteered at festivals, museums and schools. She conducts workshops for adults and children and has been a visiting freelance artist with schools and community centers during most of the past eighteen years. She has worked extensively with a wide variety of special education groups, most recently becoming involved in sculpture and building environments that involve collaboration with other artists to produce multi-media, inter-related arts performance events.

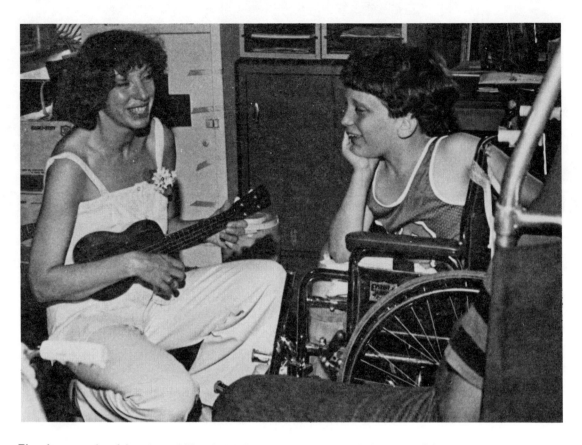

The classroom is a laboratory of life—*Judith Schwab integrates music into an activity*

A Personal Perspective

By Judith Schwab

"Our limitations can stimulate creativity." Recently this idea was expressed by Paul Winter at a music-making workshop I attended.[1] I believe Mr. Winter was speaking specifically about improvising in music and at the same time in the broader realm about life. This makes sense to me, because I have seen how the struggle with a limitation can provide motivation for solving a situation in a new way. Working with the exceptional child, one must keep this idea firmly in view. Sometimes it is the facilitator who must find the key that will circumvent a particular limitation so that a student's creativity be allowed to surface. In order to accomplish this end, we must address the spark of human spirit apparent and alive in each of us, allowing it to transcend the limitations of physical vehicle.

The classroom is a laboratory of life. As such, children must feel free to express themselves. Students can only feel free when their expression is valued. Each child has the right to feel important, respected for expressing his or her reality, for the truth is as fragile as our own reality of it. It is the teacher's job to identify abilities and guide pupils toward more fully realizing their potential with all means possible for independent study. Unimpaired children naturally express themselves, making statements through art, movement, gesture and sound. In special education, however, the need for developing a positive self-image is essential because it is sometimes more difficult to accomplish. Students—whether physically, emotionally or multi-handicapped—must gain a sense of their valued place in their community. Enhancement of their own worth can be achieved through the arts.

This concept was well illustrated during the summer of 1982 when I coordinated a community art exhibition and workshop at the Joseph H. Douglas School in Wilmington, Delaware, one of the special schools where I am a visiting artist. A Boy's Club group attended the art opening. In addition to the student art work which hung on the walls of the school I arranged for a workshop experience for our guests. These normal children took instruction from the exceptional students from the school, who had mastered certain art techniques. The visitors made puppets, did printmaking, learned rag tapestry and finger knitting. A theatre arts program was also presented with the summer school students leading the songs and performing dances. I improvised lyrics to a song, "Happy Arts Day to You," based on a melody I learned at the Paul Winter Consort music making workshop. The song reinforced the concepts that these students had learned and further helped our visitors identify student accomplishments. Our students performed beautifully in their new role as leaders. Improvement in the students' self-image was apparent by their smiles and exemplary behavior.

Puppetry is another avenue which can raise self-esteem and provide a natural focus for creative arts. It links together music, movement and environmental sounds. It can incorporate math, science, social studies, and every aspect of the modern day curriculum. After working in puppetry for eighteen years, I realize that each workshop teaches me new ways to create puppets. There is no end to ideas waiting to be discovered.

My interest is puppetry began as an adult. After college, marriage and motherhood, I helped to organize a needed recreational facility. We were building a new Y.M.C.A. branch organization in our young community of Northeast Philadelphia. After teaching myself puppetry from books and experimentation, I taught others how to develop a puppetry program. I recruited volunteers, training young women like myself to work with teenagers and campers. We used puppetry as a means to motivate "latency age" campers to become involved. As a result, they produced an original puppet show for the younger set. The show may not have been up to professional standards, but everyone enjoyed it and it identified for us a core of people who wanted to stay involved.

This activity led me to take a job in Philadelphia as an aide in the Jewish Day Nursery Mecor-Chaim. Fortunately, I assisted a teacher who encouraged me to do more than pour juice and clean tables. This experience marked the beginning of my interest and adventure with integrating media. I created songs using simple chords for a ukulele strum, which reinforced learning concepts. I developed appropriate art activities and used puppetry to tie all the subjects together. Eventually, I became a nursery school teacher, returning to college and then to graduate school for the study of creative arts.

Much of what I find valuable today, began during times of free play in my early development. I was fortunate to have attended the Settlement School of Music and Art in Philadelphia, Pennsylvania. It was there that I first experienced live classical music, which was practiced and played while I sculpted with clay and painted on paper. As a young child, it seemed natural to me that music and art belonged together. Elementary school, after the freedom of expression in kindergarten, was a great disappointment. When the large pots of paints, building blocks, freedom of movement, and dress-up corner disappeared, so too did my love of school. Teachers became directive in their style.

From this experience, I know that children learn from what is said, the way it is spoken as well as from what is not said. Much of what I consider unacceptable teaching practice, I learned from remembering my classroom experiences as a young child. If I were to identify these negative values, they would be for me: (a) the expectation of hearing only one right answer which consequently restricts individual creativity; (b) the selection of role models, children identified as teacher's pet. As an adult, I am never far from those early childhood sensibilities. Now these memories inspire me to try harder. I take as many master classes as I can in dance, music, puppetry, drama and sculpture. What prevents some of us from doing this is the fear of failure and/or non-acceptance. Children need an accepting, fail-proof environment even more than adults do. The prime factor in positive growth is to keep ourselves open to constructive change and to allow ourselves to try new things. Burn-out occurs more quickly without continual growth.

I believe growth within the exceptional child *always* takes place. Sometimes the growth is so slow it is impossible to see it charted on a weekly basis. The exceptional child grows at different rates because of marked individual differences. All information can be made more palatable with a song and/or through puppetry. I find music a valuable tool for relaxing and motivating. This is especially important when I work with pupils whose muscles are tensed from disease. Whether I make music vocally or sing with a recording, I find that it relaxes me and I, in turn, help the students to relax.

The best approach in working with all these groups is to improvise simple songs and sing them, repeating the concepts as you work, or use a recording that relates to objectives. The melodies sometimes come from the rhythm of the words in my thoughts or from my written lesson "Music is not a frill" and reinforced by the following quote.

It is time music stopped being regarded as just recreation for the handicapped. True, it is an excellent form of recreation and it is excellent therapy. Music as an educational tool can open up a whole new area in the education of handicapped students. It is a valuable teaching aid which any teacher can use. It is not necessary to have a background in music methods. Most of the games and songs are simple familiar ones. It is not necessary to play a piano. It is sometimes better not to have the obstacle of a piano between the teacher and the student.

Sherry R. Mills[2]

A dangerous thing has happened. Teaching professionals tend to think of themselves as specialists and they try to work strictly within their specialty. Something is lost here. When we become afraid to infringe on another professional's area, we inhibit the creative process in ourselves and this affects our students.

Every educator should try to be more of a Renaissance Person. It is an ideal which we, each in our own way, can attain. If creativity can be stimulated by trying to overcome a limitation, then teachers must reach beyond what they think their limitations are to artistically try new ways of communicating. How can we ever know what our limitations are if we never try to reach beyond them?

An example of how this philosophy has worked is demonstrated by my first venture into the world of sculpture, which became a multimedia event. Conceptually it was inspired by the writings of Jamake Highwater (refer to Native American article in this section), though it came about as a direct result of my attempt to reach beyond what I believe my limitations are. I have always wanted to create environments but felt overwhelmed by the idea of using tools and actually making large three dimensional structures. I have never even built my own puppet stage for this reason.

In the summer session of 1983 I enrolled in a graduate studio course with professor/sculptor Joe Moss at the University of Delaware. I began working with natural fibers, using vines, branches and rafia most of which I pulled from the woods of Delaware. A fall course enabled me to work longer and produce a related arts multimedia event—*Judith Schwab: Searching Nature.* I collaborated with two musicians and a modern dance guild integrating all the parts for a participatory art show that was received by the public.

The creative arts experience is one that blends many educational, aesthetic, sensual activities into a unified statement, such as the "Searching Nature" event mentioned. This unity can be accomplished quite effectively through puppetry, which utilizes a wide variety of media, and motivates participation.

Pedagogically speaking, we can never saturate our need for expression through sensation in the educational process. The following articles were undertaken with the idea of raising self-image through puppetry and the arts as a primary goal along with teaching art content. I am grateful for the opportunity to share these unique experiences with you.

Footnotes

[1]Paul Winter Consort Workshop, "Voices of Earth," Omega Institute, Rhinebeck, NY, August, 1982.

[2]Sherry R. Mills, "Music—the Reinforcer," *Education Unlimited,* December, 1979, P. 49. (Educational Resources Center, 1834 Meetinghouse Road, Boothuryn PA 19061.)

The magical attraction of puppetry was used to help special students express their hitherto hidden imagination—*Photo by Jim Carter of Hercules, Inc.*

Puppetry and Imagination

Funded in part by the Delaware State Arts Counsel Mini-Grant and by the Lindenhill School P.T.A.
By Judith Schwab

Every human being is born with imagination. Unfortunately, however, in education, imagination is usually equated with 'Art'; art is equated with professional practice; those children who show some degree of achievement in one or the other of the arts are labeled imaginative, and the closer their work is to the accepted criteria of 'good' professional art then the more imaginative they are. The remainder are 'no good' at art and because imagination and art are equated, are therefore 'unimaginative'. Human dignity being the bastion that it is, the majority effortlessly accepted this quality of unimaginativeness.[1]

Brian Way

This program was undertaken to reverse the attitude of viewing students who do not conform as unimaginative. The magical attraction of puppetry was used to help special students express their hitherto hidden imaginations. Bodi-Puppets were introduced with a series of interrelated multimedial activities that culminated in a performance based on the student's poetry. This imaginative and expressive process provided a positive focus for exceptional students who felt isolated from the mainstream even in mainstreamed situations. An experiment such as this not only affects those emotionally fenced in by their peer group situation, but generates new vehicles of communication for all.

Our objective was to provide one class of exceptional students, ages seven through ten and with mixed disabilities (educable mentally retarded, emotionally disturbed, and others), at the Lindenhill Elementary School in Wilmington, Delaware, with the opportunity to achieve emotional goals in socialization and language arts expression. While the study did not contain a comparison group, the subjects' attitudes and responses were noted in their teacher's informal assessment (anecdotal records). The participating teacher, Betty Klabunde, and the principal, Marvin Balick, made clear the need for these students to develop a balance between self-control and self-expression. This was to be a two-week program with students grouped together to form a newly self-contained class of thirteen students.

In a preliminary telephone conversation, Ms. Klabunde had said that her students did not enjoy art, that they were either acting up or being punished for behavioral problems in the artroom environment. By October, Ms. Klabunde had made an informal assessment of the students' potential based on behavioral observations. I was invited to visit the class, meet their teacher and later make a creative arts recommendation to tap students' innovative resource of expression. On this first visit, the high energy level I sensed, brought to mind a name game I had learned at a drama workshop with The Learning Theatre in Patterson, New Jersey. It seemed to be a perfect vehicle as a warmup and to get to know the pupils. Chairs were placed in a circle and students' names were chanted one at a time. Tapping our thighs with our palms, we created a rhythmic pattern to follow:

It began:

	Tap	*Tap*	*Tap*	*Tap*
	x	*x*	*x*	*x*
	My	*name's*	*Ju-*	*dy*

(x indicates contact with the body, patting thigh.)

Ju-dy	*Ju-dy*	*Ju-dy*
x-x	*x-x*	*x-x*

The game involved varying the rhythms and tonal patterns to communicate different messages about their names. At first, students were enthusiastic and responsive, but reluctant to initiate. However, they were most happy to imitate. The high level of energy seemed to communicate hidden creative potential.

Many months passed, while waiting for approval of the mini-grant application. In the interim, Ms. Klabunde said that students from time to time at recess were heard name chanting as we had done with our names at our first meeting.

An important indirect link between the school and the home was established when parents were asked to begin sending to school assorted scrap materials such as newspaper, old hosiery and empty detergent boxes in preparation for the project.

The Program

When Principal Balick gave official permission to begin the puppetry program, the class of thirteen was divided into three compatible social-play groups, which interestingly matched their reading levels. Reading levels varied from reading readiness to second grade. Each group attended the puppetry workshop for thirty minutes every day for a two week period. The entire program involved five hours of face to face in-person time. The total involved time for the entire program including the show, was five hours per group or fifteen hours for all three groups. While I worked alone with each one-third segment, the teacher and aide worked with the remaining two thirds segment of the class.

Attendance in the workshop became motivation for positive behavior in the classroom and for the completion of the student's regular seat work. Once rapport was established, seeing these students on successive days kept involvement going and was essential. Prior to the actual puppet activity, I set up a series of loosely knit activities to serve to warm up the group, explore feelings and build positive self-assurance.

MEETING 1—Motivate Expression

- **Introduction Music**

"Hello Song"
Each activity session began with a song. A ukulele was strummed and a song was improvised called "I Like Myself". We talked about feelings, noting the way we sometimes show one face to the outside world while we may be feeling something quite different inside.

- **Body Movement or Nonverbal Expression**

The class conveyed feelings by the way they moved their bodies. For example, I asked the students to think *anger* at me and then to gesture this emotion in any way they wished using only their hands and faces. A student expressed the concept by curling his fingers, making a claw-like hand and an angry shape with his mouth, showing teeth, while grimacing. Next, I asked how he would move with his whole body to show the same strong feeling! This was more profound and total in expression. Each student had a turn and other descriptive words were explored as model base.

- **Water Painting on a Chalk Board**

The idea of expressing emotions nonverbally with body action was extended by using a wet painter's brush with the students. First, students were asked simply to make a line on the chalkboard with the wet brush (no paint) to correspond with the emotions explored—*wild, angry* or *quiet.* "We want to make a line, not a picture of something," I conveyed. This was a deliberate attempt to have students connect an abstract symbol (line) with an emotion. The wet brush left a solid and easily recognizable streak on the board. Students were asked to wipe their brushes on the edge of the water bucket to avoid dripping.

There is something magical about water painting on chalkboard. Perhaps it is the water's ability to appear and then disappear as it dries, lacking the permanence that sometimes inhibits visual artistic expression. Whatever the reason, it had a hypnotic effect. Students seemed deeply engrossed in the artistic expression of their classmates during these spontaneous chalkboard painting sessions.

A key to having success with hyperactive students is the facilitator's ability to plan activities that change frequently. Taking students from expression that flows naturally (less demanding cognitively) to more demanding kinds of expression, such as from a nonverbal, body movement exercise to the small motor nonverbal exercise of painting as experienced in our preliminary meeting offers students opportunity to understand concepts on varying levels. Positive behavior reinforcement given often during this time is essential to the end results and cooperative efforts of individual students.

Expressing emotions nonverbally through wet painting—*Photo by James Dawson, Delaware Today Magazine*

• **Tempera Line Painting on Large Pad**

Next, students painted with primary tempera paint colors and large brushes on a large newsprint pad. They worked one at a time while group members watched. This next step was a deliberate attempt to focus attention, stretch concentration and develop respect for materials and a sense of empathy for peer accomplishment. Peer group recognition such as this can successfully begin in a very small group situation, when image raising is desired.

Instructions were similar to those given for water painting. The students were asked to choose one color that best expressed a chosen feeling. One boy chose "sad." Previously, he made a water rainbow on the chalkboard and later painted a blue rainbow with the tempera on paper. Not everyone followed through using exactly their original water painting expressive line, but they all followed through with their chosen expressive color. The students chose to express anger with the paints black or red, sadness with blue and happiness or joy with yellow paint. This color psychology was developed by the students with no direction from me as to what color to select to convey their emotions.

• **Exit With Music**

This initial half hour meeting was brought to a close with a song played again on the ukulele.

Thank you for coming in here today.
I liked the things you did and the things you
had to say.
You are so nice, you're so neat,
You make this group quite complete.

The next group was greeted with an improvised hello song.

Hello, Hello, Hello,
I am glad to meet you.
I am glad to greet you.
Hello, Hello, Hello.

MEETING 2—Relating to Puppets

• **Brainstorming (What Can A Puppet Be)**

It was appropriate that we built puppets around the idea of expressing feelings. At the outset of this meeting a link between puppets and emotions was made when students were shown a large picture of an antique native American Indian string puppet. Not only did it have a face to express emotions but it had two doors in its chest that opened to show other facial emotions. In addition it had facial expressions painted on the palms of its hands.[2] This reinforced the idea that historically primal peoples had used creative ways to show inner feelings and emotions.

The ukulele again accompanied a song I improvised called "Puppetry is an Ancient Art." The song has a brainstorming element that leads to a discussion about what you can make a puppet out of.

They tell me that puppetry is an ancient art going back to the ancient Greeks, the Chinese used puppets to entertain their kings. Puppets are happy, puppets are sad, there are good puppets and some that are very bad! Puppets are wicked, puppets are mean, puppets are the most interesting things I've ever seen.

by Judy Schwab

American Indian String Puppet with face showing emotions on chest—*Courtesy of the Museum of the American Indian. Heye Foundation*

99

• **Discussion on Noises and Sounds**

We next discussed the things that scare us to further reinforce understanding of emotional feelings. Students participated in another improvised song called "Night Noises." This song is sung to the tune of "London Bridge" with the idea of opening students to listening and becoming more aware of their environment. By listening to night sounds when they went to bed they were bringing classroom experience home and back to school the next day when they would share with the group night noises they heard.

Night Noises

by Judy Schwab

There are noises in the night,
　　　　　in the night,
　　　　　in the night.
Friendly noises don't cause fright,
my dear ___(child's name)___

There are noises when it's dark,
　　　　　when it's dark,
　　　　　when it's dark
Like trains and planes and dogs, that bark,
my dear ___(child's name)___

There are noises all about,
　　　　　all about,
　　　　　all about.
A sneeze, a wheeze, a cough, a shout,
my dear ___(child's name)___

Noises are such fun to hear,
　　　　　fun to hear,
　　　　　fun to hear.
Can you imagine giggles from a dancing bear?
my dear ___(child's name)___

Collecting noises can be done
　　　　　can be done
　　　　　can be done
When you listen to each one,
my dear ___(child's name)___

Tell me noises that you hear,
　　　　　that you hear,
　　　　　that you hear,
A growl, a wheeze, a whistle, a sneeze, a roar?
Or was it just a gentle snore?

Let's all snore and sing once more.

Night Noises is followed by an assignment.

Students are asked to listen to sounds when they go to bed at night and tell about sounds they heard in school the next day.

This opens students to their environment and should help perception if it is reinforced and repeated with other sounds, different times of the day.

• **What Can We Use to Build a Puppet?**

Students were given time to interact with my own hand puppets before making their own puppets from scrap materials. This preparatory session included focusing on the visual and tactile components of simple scrap materials. Holding my scrap puppets as examples, I asked, "What is this puppet made from?" I would point to various features such as the egg carton eyes or button nose. Also, such questions as, "How is this button attached so that it will hang properly?", provided ground for constructive thinking.

It was of interest to all when later in the project, upon exploring scrap material puppets, a student, Dawn, brought in a marvelous puppet head she created on her own from home. It had plastic cookie wrappers for eyes, a broken head band mouth and a half of a L'Egg panty hose container nose and was fastened entirely with scotch tape. It was a clever design with two paper plates taped together so that the back paper plate face was hidden behind the front paper plate face. The front face had a broad smiling expression and the back hidden face (Dawn let me see) had huge tears and a sad expression with large sad eyes. Dawn's achievement in independent creativity was recognized.

MEETING 3 to 7—Making the Puppets

The third meeting of this segment consisted of all thirteen students working together to build the puppet heads that would later be attached to the Bodi-Puppets. The heads were constructed from Paris Craft bandages (a form of plaster of Paris obtained from art supply stores) over bases of paper plates. The plaster dried overnight enabling students to paint them the following day.

Each meeting involving puppetmaking began and ended with the songs already mentioned. The remaining two meetings were used to complete the Bodi-Puppets, creating the body and arms and legs.

During these sessions students had opportunities to become intimate in exploring a rich selection of scrap materials for applying to the puppets' bodies and

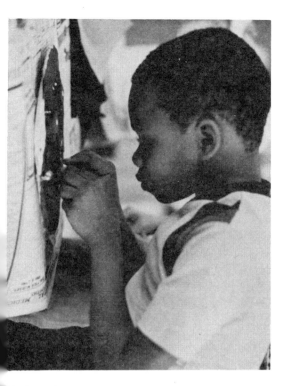

Students becoming intimate with materials while constructing Bodi-Puppets—*Photo by Jim Carter*

costumes such as cellophane, sequins, rick rack and the like. Touching, squeezing, pulling and blowing were a few ways students could interact intimately with these materials. This was done in conjunction with seeing the corresponding vocabulary words lettered on the chalkboard. We took the time in class to sound out each syllable of these words: sequin, cellophane, yarn, etc. If students were unfamiliar with the words, they were encouraged to guess at the pattern of the letters to make that abstract connection between symbol and object.

MEETING 8—Creative Dramatics

• **Creative Dramatics**

Once the Bodi-Puppets were complete, we began the creative dramatics portion of our program mainly to warm up the students prior to the show experience. Daily positive group experience built student confidence and led to an atmosphere of creative expression. This was achieved in part by using Teacher Effectiveness Training Techniques,[3] such as active listening and positive social behavior reinforcment (i.e., "I like the way Katrina is sitting, ready to work"). Some exercises were selected from Brian Way's *Development Through Drama* and Rosilyn Wilder's *A Space Where Anything Can Happen*.[4]

One of the three groups responded to Way's and Wilder's exercises while a second group did not relate

to any of these exercises but responded to my "Guided Fantasy" and acted out the story which follows.

One rainy day, as I left the supermarket, I stepped onto the parking lot. Suddenly I noticed hundreds of colors that looked like swirling puddles of paint covering the parking lot. As I stepped into one of the puddles, my foot got caught in a color and I was pulled into the sky. Somehow you (the students) were there with me. Then, we were all floating around the sky surrounded by color!

Students took liberties to change my fantasy which was abstract and brought it back to a concrete reality. When I asked them what color was closest to us, Aaron said, "Orange." As we were floating in orange, Aaron said, "I found an orange." He was forming a cup with his hand showing that he was holding something round in his palm like an orange. Tom pulled the imagined orange from Aaron's hand and repeated, "I found an orange." This was repeated till the last person said, "I'm going to eat it, too!" I told

101

someone to think of a way to stop him from eating it. Then each person thought of a reason for the person not to eat it when it was their turn.

The third group (reading readiness level) responded to none of these exercise approaches. However, this group showed great originality in creating poems and stories that appear at the end of this section about their puppets. It is important for the instructor in working with special children to recognize that when an idea does not connect the first time, it is a signal to try a new approach. Often the connection is made because the psychological chemistry is right at the moment.

• Related Activities

The music teacher, Terry Duke, was teaching songs that related directly to the concerns of these children—"Everybody Needs a Friend" and "There's No One in The World Like Me."[5] This was an opportunity to relate another subject area to our creative arts experience. Ms. Duke agreed to accompany the students on the piano using these songs for our show in addition to the poems we planned to use. She not only found a way to help us, which was in addition to her normal busy schedule, she also gave valuable direction, organization and played background music.

The Performance

In order to make these special education students comfortable for their performance we tried to eliminate the sight of an audience. This was done by darkening the room. Students performed in the same colored light they had chosen to express their emotional feelings earlier. This was accomplished with a film strip projector with colored acetate over the projector light. It was also here that we began to integrate the completed puppets. We saved the actual wearing of the puppets for the day of the performance, due to the fact that some of the students' attention spans were short or that some students would not tolerate wearing puppets longer than was absolutely necessary. However, in the process of creating them, they seemed to have internalized their puppets' personalities and did not need to wear them in the preliminary creative dramatics exercises in order to relate to them. The puppets, as it turned out, served primarily as a mask of emotional protection from which to elude their peers on the day of the performance.

The dress rehearsal was actually our first perfor-

mance. These children did not have the patience required to perfect a performance through practice. Acceptance of the charm of successful imperfection and spontaneity is the key here.

A stage-like effect was created in our classroom by hanging white draperies (sheets can also be used) borrowed from home. They were draped over a pole that was suspended between two school room panel dividers, forming a half moon shape. The performance was done in semi-darkness with an eerie colored light shone from a film strip projector. The light illuminated the Bodi-Puppets as they came to center stage.

Some students needed a reassuring hand to hold as I guided them to center stage. One boy refused to perform wearing his puppet, and another simply refused to perform period! Thus, having a puppet to hide behind for eleven of these thirteen children in the semi-darkness made this a successful experiment. From personal childhood experience, this writer understands how anxiety and low self-esteem can produce the kind of fear of failure that immobilizes the human spirit.

As our audience (both handicapped and nonhandicapped) began to enter the classroom, the tension began to mount. The incoming groups were a good audience. They sat cross-legged Indian style in a half circle. Wearing Bodi-Puppets, our performers were seated on chairs on opposite sides of the mini-stage. The music teacher with her piano and a music class were there. Adding to the mood, the original tempera line-paintings that the students had done expressing feelings at our first meeting were displayed on the walls of the classroom.

An easel with the story and poems created by the performing children was displayed in large letters with colored markers. This tablet faced the student audience. Colored streamers for decoration hung below the display tablet. The film strip projector for lighting effect was in place facing the center stage area and one tape recorder with audio portion was hooked up. It contained the students' two songs, the skit "I Found an Orange" and the poems that follow. We also had a slide projector ready to show the process of how the Bodi-Puppets were made after the presentation. During the program the songs were sung live with the tape recorder leading, then students wearing Bodi-Puppets dramatized the poems as they were played on the tape. Lastly everyone watched the slides that showed how the entire project was accomplished.

One week later we did the show again for the entire school on the auditorium-gymnasium stage. Parents, administrators from the Delaware State Arts Council and school personnel were attending. It was a success!

Assembled performers singing "Everybody Needs a Friend"—*Photo by Jim Carter*

Summary of Program

Ms. Klabunde reported that before this program took place, students were isolated from their peers even in mainstreamed situations. Her students were treated like untouchables by their peers. If there was any contact, it was usually negative in nature. She said further, that for weeks after this show was performed, regular and gifted students were speaking to her pupils, asking questions and giving positive feedback such as the following:

That was a neat show you did.
Was that really your voice I heard?
How did you make those big puppets?
I never thought you could do anything like that.

Principal Balick, was pleased with the results and said, "The Puppetry and Imagination program was a definite help in raising the self-image of these children."

Betty Klabunde should be recognized for her efforts above and beyond what one might think possible in dedication and support of this program. While this writer had second thoughts from time to time about having the students actually perform a show, Ms. Klabunde's faith in her students never waivered! She provided both physical and moral support.

A local newspaper article appeared with a photograph taken the day of the first rehearsal-show. Weeks later, students showed me the tattered remains of their names printed in the newspaper article which they still carried in their pockets.

Psychologists, counselors and teachers who work with special children can often be limited by their own imaginations. This detailed description of Ms. Schwab's program can serve as a basis for encouraging professionals to experiment with more creative methods of effective education. The comments quoted from regular education and gifted students suggest that the

103

program sparked positive reaction toward special students.

Jane Weirekbach-Holt, Psychologist
Sterck School For The Hearing Impaired

Without the donated photographic documentation done by Jim Carter of Hercules, Inc. and James Dawson of *Delaware Today Magazine*, the programs presented in this book might not have been possible.

Footnotes

[1]Brian Way, *Development Through Drama* (Atlantic Highlands, N.J.: Humanities Press, 1973), p. 42.

[2]Bil Baird, *The Art of the Puppet* (New York: Bonanza Books, 1973), p. 29.

[3]Project T.E.A.C.H. 175 Westwood Avenue, Westwood, New Jersey 07675.

[4]Rosilyn Wilder, *A Space Where Anything Can Happen*.

[5]Don Dinkmeyer, *DUSO Kit, Level D-2* (Developing Understanding of Self and Others) American Guidance Service, Publishers Building, Circle Pines, MN 55014.

To Make Plaster Craft Head for Bodi-Puppet.

Head Section

Materials: Paris craft bandage strips (obtained at craft shop); water; paper plate; rope; large buttons, styrofoam packaging pieces; empty film or L'egg hosiery containers; egg carton sections and other odds and ends.

Construction: Lay paper plate flat on table and build up a face design with odds and ends: egg carton sections or L'egg containers make excellent eyes; rope can be curved into a mouth design; and buttons or other items used for a nose. Strips of masking tape can be used to secure items to plate.

Precut plastercraft strips into 5 inch lengths.

Put water in a dishpan type container and dip plaster strips as you use them in water. Lay each wet strip over surface of plate, covering facial relief design. Put on enough strips to cover entire face.

Let face dry and paint with tempera paint.

Have students write the name of their chosen emotion on the back of the plate and name of color that expressed their emotion.

Body Section

Refer to the basic Bodi-Puppet construction on page 59 for making body. Also an alternate head design is offered of an easier construction for less advanced projects.

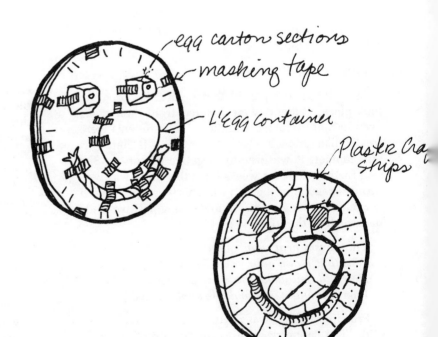

egg carton sections
masking tape
L'egg container
Plaster craft strips

THE POEMS

The following poems were improvised by the students and captured on a tape recorder as they said the words with this author acting as facilitator.

All About An Orange

(4) *I found an orange.*
(2) *I found an orange.*
(3) *I found an orange.*
(1) *I found an orange,*
   and I'm gonna eat it!

(3) *Don't eat it, its sour!*
(2) *Don't eat it, its poison!*
(4) *Don't eat it, its dirty!*
(1) *I'm gonna eat it anyway!*

(2) *I saw it fall on the ground!*
(3) *I saw somebody lick it!*
(4) *It's my orange and*
   I'm taking it back!

Number before line indicates the speaker. by (1) Tom Lilly, (2) Jeanette Davis, (3) Angela Curtis and (4) Aaron Turner.

My Funny Goose

My Funny Goose is six years old.
The worst thing Funny Goose has to do
is to make people laugh!

By Tracey Farrow

The Creature From
The Black Lagoon

He is green.
He is mean.
He doesn't like strangers.
He is ugly.
He is wild.
He doesn't like people.
He is rough.
He is tough.
He doesn't like me!

By James Dwayne Tolliver

Puppetry and Imagination

by Katrine Scarborough
Renee Panacione
Edward Neal
Valerie Daniels
Gregory Carter

Once upon a time,
in the scary land of dreams,
there was a ghost and a witchmonster
and a pig.

They had no other
friends. They were
lonesome. The ghost began to cry.

The witchmonster wants to make the ghost
feel better. He asks the pig to help.
The pig says, "Finding new friends
is easy, all you have to do is look."
"We will all look," says the witch-
monster. All of a sudden a measles
chicken face pox bumps appears!
"Where did you come from,"
asks the ghost?
The measles chicken face pox bumps says,
"I am from Wilmington, and I'm glad
to have new friends."

The dream sequence in Dicken's Christmas Carol was the perfect vehicle for the Op Art puppetry with its emphasis on shapes, colors, movement and creative expression—*Photo by Judith Schwab*

Dream Sequence Puppets

By Judith Schwab

Moving to Delaware created new opportunities for this writer to become involved in a program for trainable* and severely mentally handicapped students, sponsored jointly by the self-contained Charles W. Bush Public School and the New Castle County Department of Parks and Recreation Special Populations Section. The Bush School had many wonderful support services, but art was not one of them. Inviting a visiting artist brought enrichment to the school's already excellent educational setting and it provided substance in developing leisure-time interests for students. One day each week, for a duration of ten weeks, I would "float" from classroom to classroom, working with each class for about twenty minutes.

This was my first experience working in a self-contained educational setting for mentally impaired students. In a self-contained school all students in school are handicapped whereas in a regular school the special education students are sometimes in self-contained classrooms and other times mainstreamed into classroooms with nonhandicapped students. Input from teachers was sought in the self-contained setting and after discussion, it was suggested that a reinforcement of learning the concept of shapes and colors would help support their program. After much thought, an art program was adopted that had been previously developed for a heterogeneous middle school, entitled, "An Op Art Puppetry Experience." This particular Op Art activity was presented to two trainable classes. The goal was to strengthen abstract concepts, teach new vocabulary, provide skill in making puppets, and develop an understanding of artists' lives, leading to a multi-media interdisciplinary performance through puppetry.

Two groups were selected to experience this Op Art puppetry adventure. To determine how a range of students with varying abilities would respond, one group was considered high level and the other classified as a lower level trainable class (high level students had basic reading skills, low level did not). This article presents the work of the higher level class in detail. Each session met for 25 minutes per day. The objectives for the program were as follows:

- Motivation through individual student reponses to Op Art works shown on slides.
- Creation and understanding of geometric designs using templates and complementary colors, (i.e. red-green, blue-orange, yellow-purple).
- Transforming the art work into moveable hand puppets.
- A final performance by the students using puppets to the music "The Emperor's March" that was part of the dream sequence from the school's holiday production of *A Christmas Carol*, by Charles Dickens.

In preliminary preparation, 35mm slides were made by photographing from an exhibition catalog obtained by the Wilmington Free Library (Concord Branch) called *The Responsive Eye*, a collection of Op Art works documented by the Museum of Modern Art, New York City, in the '60's. The students' chief motivation came from these slides. They were shown only three slides each week during the first five sessions, making a total of fifteen slides. Because the children were shown relatively few slides over a wide span of time, it gave them a better opportunity to absorb the material as it was reinforced weekly.

The Program

As I focus on the process involved during this ten meeting session, I will be describing the learning process of this trainable class of eight high level students, ranging in age from twelve to sixteen. We began the entire project in early October and it culminated in December, with the holiday dream sequence show.

At our first meeting, the students in the class were shown the three initial Op Art slides. We spent at least five minutes discussing each slide in the beginning. This was followed by giving students class time to match colors and shapes they saw in clothing people were wearing and in their classroom environment. This helped to strengthen the students' connection between the slide elements of design and their own clothing. These were some of the questions that

107

were asked of the students about the slides.

- *What colors do you see?*
- *What lines do you see?*
- *Can you touch or trace these lines with your hand?*
- *Are the lines wavy or straight?*
- *Can you make a line on our chalkboard like the line shown on the slide?*
- *Where can we find straight lines in this room?*
- *Is there a line that we can see repeated?*

The project itself was broken down into several stages after this initial introduction with slides.

• Creating the Op Art Designs

We then discussed the idea of making designs similar to the ones we saw. The one inch block graph paper used in rug hooking was offered because regular architect's graph paper was too small in scale. As it turned out, even with the large grid, most students had difficulty seeing the pale blue lines and were not able to choose which shapes they wished to emphasize.

They also had difficulty coloring in the one inch squares since some students had fine motor coordination problems. I decided instead to offer geometrically shaped cardboard templates so that they could have flexible creative options in designing their art. These templates had the shapes cut out of the middle to facilitate use by students with motor coordination difficulties. Toward this effort, many more shapes had to be provided than were actually needed in order to present enough possibilities of combinations. Students enjoyed tracing the templates and coloring inside the traced shapes. They also created interesting designs with squares within squares, rectangles within rectangles and circles within circles. Other template solutions were found, such as the templates that house yogurt containers to keep them from spilling while in transit.

After completion of the initial designs, the students were familiarized with the elements of basic shapes. They were then exposed to the works of Joseph Albers and Bridget Riley in addition to the slides we used and they became familiar with Albers' series "Homage to the Square." A poster of "Homage to the Square," a geometric design by Albers, was hung on the wall in the classroom for reinforcement. Watercolor markers in complementary colors were now added for the introduction of color. To reinforce the concept and enhance the overall effect, students were allowed to use complementary colors only, because these color complements, when juxtaposed, seemed to vibrate, thus causing the optical effect that is characteristic of Op Art. When students were shown works from slides or from books, they were given the basic facts about the artists' lives. In the process, they were constantly encouraged to verbalize their feelings and ideas.

• Introducing Vocabulary Concepts

Just before the end of the third session, the word *vertical* was introduced. It was written on the chalkboard and I pronounced it in clear syllables, "ver-ti-cal." The students were asked, "Does anyone know what this means?" This discussion was followed by the class being asked to stand, then told, "We are all standing like the trees, like the door. We are standing vertical." Then students were requested to find other vertical lines in their classroom environment. References were also made to their home environment with such statements as, "When we get out of bed in the morning, we stand up vertical." A homework assignment was to have students "think" of themselves as being "vertical" like the trees. Students were asked, "Who can stand vertical like me?" "Who can make a vertical line on our chalkboard?" Many more ways were found for similar active participation activities. The work went slowly but steadily, moving and gradually improving.

During the fifth meeting, the antonym "horizontal" was introduced. Similarly, we found horizontal lines on the slides and horizontal elements in the classroom such as becoming "horizontal" by lying on the floor. Homework was assigned: Students were asked to think about being "horizontal" when they were in bed at night. I told them, "I sleep horizontal just as you do." Each week the vertical/horizontal concept was reinforced with variation. Each group of slides brought new chances to find vertical and horizontal lines or movements and identify them along with other concepts.

• Op Art Puppets

Since students were preparing the puppet project for their Christmas show, I purchased Christmas garlands in hopes that they would enjoy using them for arms, legs and other puppet parts. The basic Op Art designs, made with templates and complementary colors were glued to oak tag paper for rigidity. A 3-inch wide styrofoam strip was cut from packaging material and glued onto the center of the puppet's back for support. When students decided that their puppets needed a head, they used paper plates. Some made antennas to add to the head with strips of paper which were trimmed off their original Op Art

Students found a way to make each puppet unique — *Photo by Judith Schwab*

designs. The students found a way to make each puppet unique; some had two legs, others had four legs, and other variations.

Interrelated Activities

Various departments in the school participated in making this an exciting interrelated project. Students in other classes enjoyed creating and painting scenery for the different scenes in the performance, using moveable folding screen panels. The Home Economics Department also took an interest in our project and did an excellent job dyeing men's long sleeve business shirts so that students would be matched yet inconspicuous, and the puppets would indeed be the center of interest. Although we were using black dye, the deepest color we could achieve was a dark gray; however, the overall impression was effective. The shirts were donated by a local cleaning store. They were unclaimed long sleeve shirts.

The music selected, "The Emperor's March" from the film, *The Emperor Strikes Back*, had a strong beat, but Esther Bergstrom, the instructional aide, slowed the beat to accommodate our youngsters. We were fortunate to have her talents at the piano available to us.

After the puppets were completed, we began practicing our dance. Claire Dunigan, the choral director and classroom teacher, asked what I wanted the students to do. I explained my vision of the dance. First we spent time blocking out the dance steps, then the puppets' movements. The classroom teacher decided to give each student a number since students were accustomed to assigned numbers from gym class. A dance pattern was created and two numbers were called at a time as a cue. Students initially formed two lines of four each, facing the audience. They marched out in front of the audience while holding their puppets, then turned their backs to the audience. The two center people then turned to the front, took one large step forward, and marched away from each other, still facing the audience, to the steady marching beat. When they reached the end of the line, they marched back to the front again. Finally, taking one large step back into place, they turned their backs to the audience making their puppets seem to disappear. First, students practiced this choreographed patterning just holding their puppets. Once they had mastered the blocking movement of their bodies, we choreographed the actual movements of their puppets. As they moved apart facing the audience, they raised their puppets to the steady marching beat. First, puppets went high, high, high. Then low, low, low, now back into place, turning backs to audience, making room for the next group. All movements and directions were kept simple. Students seemed to watch each other out of the corner of their eyes to check formation and see if they were lined up with their partners. They accomplished this activity in perfect unison, resulting in excellent reinforcement of body coordination skills and group rhythm.

This large motor activity was utilizing their intellect (memorizing what to do), their sense of timing (fostering awareness of being in sync with what others were doing) and following directions. In addition, they had learned to coordinate movement to music and trained new muscle groups. Students seemed to enjoy practicing and they were most cooperative throughout the process.

Summary of Project

Students took great pride in their puppets which were indeed quite beautiful. Their sparkling quality was enhanced by the geometric foil accents, color coordination, animated arms and legs and bright Christmas garlands. This Op Art experience was a completely successful creative addition to the school's adaptation of *A Christmas Carol*.

"The dream sequence in Dicken's *Christmas Carol* was the perfect vehicle for the Op Art puppetry with its emphasis on shapes, colors, movement and creative expression," says Dunigan.

The parents and friends who support the school through the P.T.A. found a way to make the students know they appreciated their contribution at a reception held after the performance, in addition to the applause.

Just as important, students learned to make a simple puppet which could provide constructive leisure interests in the future. Furthermore, developing a new skill and performing in front of an audience helped elevate students' feelings of self-worth and therefore, their enjoyment of the whole project.

The therapeutic/recreational aspects of this project were enhanced by providing creative avenues of expression, thus exercising the senses, and making students active participants rather than passive viewers. This kind of recreational/educational activity can be most successfully done during the school day, when students are rested and at their peak, energy wise, rather than attempting it as an after school program. Dunigan's and Bergstrom's contributions were both considerable and necessary in cooperation with this project, since my contribution was limited to one 35-minute classroom visit per week.

It was gratifying to see the rapport which developed over the ten week period. As an outsider to students, it was an enrichment for them, as well as for myself, to get to know each other through the vehicle of the puppet and the ensuing production.

I encourage parks and recreation programs for the special populations to make matching in-school funds available for therapeutic/recreational activities in educational settings. I would like to thank the school's principal, Linda Mazepink, who realizes the value of the arts in her curriculum and tries to provide them on a high level.

Definition of Trainable Mentally Handicapped: I.Q. score and Adaptive Behavior score shall range between 35 to 55 I.Q. points; can learn to talk and communicate; can learn elementary health habits; can learn academic skills to approximately 3rd grade level; profits from systematic habit training. (Definition obtained through Linda Mazepink, principal, Charles W. Bush Public School, Wilmington, Delaware.)

Footnotes

Albers, Joseph. *Homage to the Square* poster. United States Postal Service (donated), 1980.

de Sawsemarez, Maurice. *Bridget Riley*. Greenwich: New York Graphic Society, 1970.

Greenberg, Pearl. *Children's Experiences in Art*. New York: Van Nostrand Reinhold, 1966.

Metropolitan Museum of Art. *Albers*. New York: Metropolitan Museum of Art, 1971.

Sterling, Carol. *Puppetry for the Classroom*. East Orange, New Jersey: Educational Improvement Center, 1965.

To Make Op Art Puppet

Materials: Paper plate; styrofoam food packaging; drawing paper; oak tag or poster board; paper fasteners; elastic or rubber bands; two-foot cording or ribbon; foil paper (red-green, blue/orange, yellow-purple); and Christmas garland and tinsels (optional).

Construction: Using templates draw and color an Op Art design directly on paper.

Glue Op Art design to oak tag or poster board backing for basic puppet's body.

Attach 5-inch wide styrofoam strip to vertical length of puppet's body on back by means of paper fasteners for reinforcement.

Attach and loop rubber band around paper fasteners in center of puppet's back as shown for hand grip.

Create a face on paper plate with coloring medium or scrap paper and attach to body section.

Scrap aluminum foil or colored foil paper can be cut into shapes and glued to surface of Op Art design for shiny accents.

Add Christmas garland or pleated paper arms and legs.

Attach neck ribbon to top of body section to tie to child's neck.

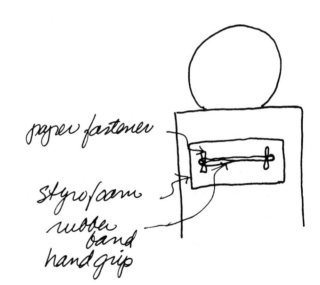

paper fastener

styrofoam

rubber band

hand grip

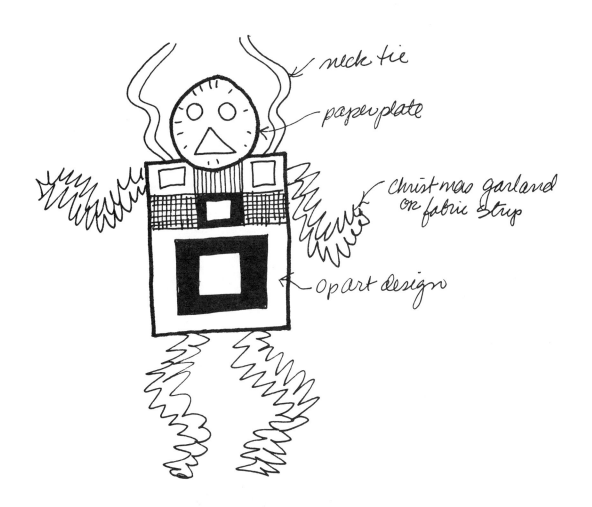

neck tie

paper plate

christmas garland
or fabric strip

op art design

Students are put in touch with primal beginnings through this display of Kachina String Puppets and Indian Name projects—*Photo by Jamie Winder*

Native American Culture for Hearing Impaired

By Judith Schwab

Have you ever been affected by the views of a speaker who has changed the way you perceived ideas? In October of 1978, I attended the Art Educators of New Jersey Convention at which the keynote speaker was art critic, anthropologist, author, native American, Jamake Highwater.

At the time I was a full time art teacher, working with third through fifth grades. Perhaps it was the combination of personal events leading to my attendance at the luncheon, as well as the content of the material, that made such an impact. A year earlier I worked as a museum docent for a native American Art Exhibition where I guided tour groups through native American artifacts, often using folk tales to illustrate how these objects of beauty evolved from a particular civilization, showing the relevence of these ideas today.

This presentation greatly influenced me in shaping the project which I describe in this section. Highwater spotlighted historically the real danger in our society's attempting, through education, to assimilate our ethnological differences into a compliant social harmony. For illustrative purposes, he used the struggle of native Americans to retain their heritage, speaking from both a personal and a historic focus. He spoke about the values of art to all mankind and said that art is an urgent necessity to all primal people.[1] As I listened to Highwater, I recognized a strong connection between the ideas that developed from my work and his views.

Highwater quoted Carl Jung and mentioned his writings as a source of understanding native American culture and our modern dilemma. Sometime later, I read Jung's book *Man and His Symbols* and found this passage written by Dr. Joseph Henderson, one of Jung's associates. "We read the myths of folk stories of American Indians, but we fail to see any connection between them and our attitudes to the 'heroes' or dramatic events of today. Yet the connections are there and the symbols that represent them have not lost their relevance for mankind."[2]

I adapted these basic ideas to help students make the connection between the mythical heroes in folk tales and events important to students today. These experiences led to the creative arts program which was developed for education enrichment in native American culture and was designed to put us in touch with our primal beginnings.

Orientation and Project Goals

As a visiting artist in 1981-82, I had a preliminary meeting with the language arts supervisor at the Margaret S. Sterck School for the Hearing Impaired located in Newark, Delaware. She introduced me to language arts teacher Liz Walker who arranged for me to observe and work with her students. Advanced II was a group of hearing impaired high school students, ranging in age from twelve to fourteen, who were bright and creative, but seemed aloof and difficult to motivate.

Liz Walker was interested in building vocabulary, language expression, abstract concepts and positive attitudes. "Hearing impaired students are often behind their hearing peers," said Walker, "in language development and overall worldliness such as general knowledge and social skills."

Because hearing impaired students need to accept differences among their peer group, as well as develop a sense of identity with others, we felt the study of American Indian culture would be helpful since it demonstrates that we can all be different, yet equal. We continued to draw on the concepts of Highwater to reinforce the program.

Jamake Highwater writes: "If we can accept the paradox that the real humanity of people is understood through differences rather than cultural similarities, then we can make profound sense of our differences. It is possible that there is not one truth but many; not one real experience but many realities; not one history, but many different and valid ways of looking at events."[3]

Highwater gives an example of this *different* but *equal* philosophy with reality being in the eyes of the beholder. For instance, native Americans see and describe a floating island with defoliated trees, while Americans see the same vision but describe it as a ship

113

with wooden masts. Who is right? Who is to judge which interpretation is more fitting? In art, as well as in other spheres, each interpretation grows out of the viewer's environment and culture. Native Americans invest all inanimate objects with an animate life; therefore what is a ship, if not a floating island with defoliated trees? Reason is not the search for truth, but rather the search for meaning. Meaning and truth are different entities and must be held as such.[4]

Highwater writes, "Children of the dominant society are rarely given the opportunity to know the world as others know it. Therefore they come to believe that there is only one world, one reality, one truth—the one they personally know; and they are inclined to dismiss all other worlds as illusions."[5]

The Meetings

After Liz Walker and I had discussed her goals and the excerpts outlined by Highwater, we began to tailor activities and projects which would be beneficial for children at Sterck School and to develop methods for presenting the material to the class.

Sterck employs a program called "total communication," which is characterized by using every creative means to get the message across. Arlene Finochiarro, Occupational Therapist Registered, in an occupational therapy publication explains it this way: "A total communication approach incorporates the use of sign language. Starting from infancy, deaf students must develop prolonged visual attention and visual concentration to attend to combined verbal and sign language communication. Additional visual skills are required for perception of sign language." Furthermore, she adds that "sign language communication comes from both sides of the brain and artistic experience is a necessary support because art trains both sides of the brain to bring the visual and language concepts together."[6] In the classroom for the hearing impaired, we observed communication taking place through finger spelling, body language, signing, speech, writing and even drawing.

At our first meeting, slides were shown of a variety of native American artifacts. A questioning technique was used to pull responses from these creative students, with the school providing an interpreter who signed my words to the students. Signing made eye contact difficult since most students, of necessity, were looking at the interpreter and not at me. However, some students had hearing aids and others seemed to be trying to read my lips.

In my initial attempt to reach the students, I focused on a shirt, made from hides, created by the Blackfeet tribe. Students appreciated the beautiful uneven natural shape of the shirt, whose surface decoration was designed to enhance the natural shape of the hide. Students recognized repeated shapes and forms that related to the earth, shapes which included circular suns, triangular mountain-like shapes, and the like. Then we collectively located the diverse cultures of native American tribes on a slide projection of a map. It was here that we saw where the Blackfeet lived.[7]

At a later session, I played songs of the Blackfeet tribe and used a special microphone and hearing device to amplify the recordings for the class. These songs were recorded in an open field in Montana on metal discs in the late 1800's and early 1900's. There were released on a Ethnic Folkway Record FE #34001 record by the Museum of Natural History in Washington, D.C. I tried to set the scene by first playing a record of rural sounds such as birds and crickets in an open field. It is impossible to report what the students actually heard. Next the slow, rhythmic beat and the chanting of the Blackfeet was played. The second time the songs were played, students kept beat to the mellow, rhythmic music by gently tapping desks with palms.

In our classes, we attempted to promote the acceptance of divergent ways of thinking as well as the acceptance of a student's expressed reality. During the motivation segment of each class, we placed chairs in a circular pattern to facilitate discussion. We spent an entire class period discussing values we believed native American cultures shared with one another, values such as their relationship to animals, the earth and the sky and other objects in nature. These conclusions were drawn from the students' own observation of artifacts they had seen through the slides, ideas expressed by Jamake Highwater, and their own life experiences.

Several interrelated activities which were used in the project are described in some detail. While these activities were geared for hearing impaired high school students, the construction methods could be adapted for younger children or general education groups.

• Indian Name Project

The considerable time spent on motivation and discussion of native American values contributed greatly to the intensity of interest inspired by the skins they created. After discussion of native American values was complete, students then chose native American names, which were used to identify their work throughout the project. During the weeks that followed, students created animal-like skins with brown paper grocery bags on which they made

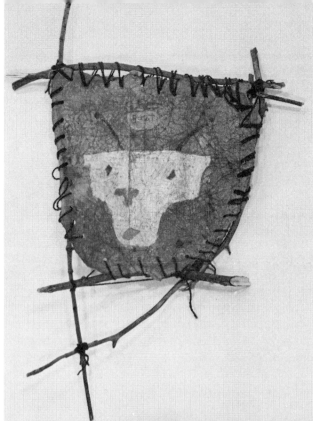

colorful designs that conveyed their names pictorially. The project was conducted in five forty-five minute work sessions.

To Make Name Design Skin

Materials: Large supermarket bag; crayons; twigs; tissue paper; watercolor paint; oak tag or poster board; and twine or leather strips.

Construction: *Session 1*—Tear out a shape on one side of a brown paper grocery bag to make the edge or shape interesting enough to resemble an animal skin or hide. Crumple, pound or stamp on paper, then smooth it out. Repeat process several times until paper has hundreds of tiny soft lines on its surface. Create a center of interest on the paper by drawing a descriptive picture that shows who you are. (Native American name). For example: "Brown Tree," "White Cloud," Blossoming Flower," Running Deer," or "Flying Eagle."

Session 2—Color surface of bag heavily with layers of waxed crayons, gradually building up the density of the wax. Create repeated patterns forming designs around the center of interest drawing such as a brown bear, green plant, white clouds, blossoming flower and running deer. Polish crayon waxed areas with a piece of tissue paper as you would polish a surface with a chamois to give it a sheen.

Session 3—Paint mock paper skin with a layer of one shade of water color paint. Allow to dry thoroughly. Mount paper skin on board for rigidity and

punch holes all around the outer edge of the skin.

Session 4—Find twigs large enough to extend 5 inches beyond any skin. Slightly sand branches to remove loose bark. Tie branches together with twine or leather to form a frame as shown.

Session 5—Attach skins to frame using brown or natural colored twine. Overcast stitches around the outside of the frame to secure. Framed mock animal skin is now ready for hanging.

The finished piece helped reinforce the concepts learned during the process, which were:

1) Respect is given to all things in nature.
2) As human beings we all have an untapped primal artist within, which —when allowed to surface—serves to help enrich our lives.

• **Introducing Native American Folk Tales**

During the first three sessions of the project, I integrated folk tales I had used in my museum work. They were short, exciting, and evoked lively visual images. Each week during this period, a folk tale was presented from a different Indian culture. The students saw slides of the works of these people and wrote compositions responding to the folk tales. "The Hunter and the Eagle" is an example of a folk tale from Northeast America. This simple tale with a focus on a strong character, the eagle, sustained students' interest for a much longer tale later in the program. The use of a repeated theme was a definite link for strengthening language. As I read the tale, it was translated into sign language. I read "The Hunter and the Eagle" just as it was retold by Burland in *North American Indian Mythology*.[8] This is my short synopsis of the tale:

THE HUNTER AND THE EAGLE

The hunter who hunts and eats deer uses magic to trick eagles so that he can steal their feathers; the mother eagle punishes the hunter by transporting him to its nesting place high in the trees. The hunter ties the baby eagles beaks closed so they cannot eat. When the Mother Eagle returns to nest with food for her babies she makes a bargain with the hunter if he will untie the beaks. The eagle offers to return the hunter to earth if he promises never again to trick an eagle. The hunter agrees and that is how the eagle is given safety to come and eat, when a deer is eaten today.

The following quotations represent the essence of

the students' responses immediately upon completion of the folk tale:

Blossoming Flower (student's Indian name)
The image of the hunter who shot the deer and ate the meat and then began to look for another was a strong image. (signed)

Brown Bear
That was a smart mother who bargained with the hunter. The hunter was also smart to tie the baby's beaks. That did not hurt the babies but it gave him bargaining power so that the eagle mother would put him down. (signed and spoken)

White Cloud
I liked the way the Indian killed the bird and cooked it with fire. A different way of life. (signed and partially spoken)

Running Deer
I liked to picture the deer in my mind as it ran into the trees. (signed and partially spoken)

- **Kachina Puppet Project**

We next studied the Kachina culture of the Hopi Indians as a means of heightening interest in this aspect of American history. The study culminated in students creating Kachina doll marionettes or string puppets.

The Kachina dolls were originally used to teach Hopi children the sacred Kachina dances. In studying the topic, students learned about the Hopi's search for cottonwood tree roots, in the face of terrible difficulties. Since women are excluded from the Kachina ceremony which deals with the supernatural, they are given Kachina dolls. Dolls are made by relatives of Indian girls and women and are often hung in their homes so as to be easily seen.[9]

Kachina dolls were created from styrofoam cups and balls and a paper mache technique in our classroom to resemble marionettes. Monofilament or fishing line string was used for manipulation. No attempt was made to imitate or copy the traditional Kachinas; rather, students created their own independent designs. We used, as our model for construction, an Asian Indian string puppet.[10] It proved an excellent choice because of quick assembly, ease of construction and the fine movement that can be achieved with a single string control. Once the Kachina marionettes were completed, students became interested in the visual effects they could achieve by simply moving their puppets by the single

Asian Indian and child made Kachina string puppet examples
Photo by Meteja Photography   *Photo by Judith Schwab*

string. This puppet activity reinforced the concept of investing inanimate materials with a spiritual essence, as did the Hopi Indians with their Kachina dolls.

Using the Puppets

Once the puppets were assembled, students choreographed their own performances, either alone or working in groups, responding to the rhythmic sounds of recordings or to sounds of their own making. Students were also given the option of using sounds from records they heard earlier in the program. With special hearing equipment, some students were able to hear sounds while moving the puppets through space. Performances were limited to two minutes. All students were able to create a visual statement by moving their string puppets. Their visual puppetry statement was largely improvised as they activated their Kachinas within their classroom peer group.

Reinforcing Concepts

During the months of weekly meetings that followed, a central theme—that of nature and man's relationship to the earth—was reinforced.[11] Through lectures and pictures, we learned that Picasso was influenced by the exciting shapes and forms in African masks, which were, in turn, influenced by shapes in nature. African art, in this way, helped usher in the expression of a new kind of modern art, cubism. We were reminded that just as everything for the native American begins and ends with the earth, so does the creative movement in the dances of Martha Graham. We learned that native Americans "listen" to rocks in Arizona with sensory skills that have nothing to do with sound, for these rocks sing and speak to our unconscious spirit when we choose to let them. This idea of hearing and listening *without sound waves* made a strong impression on these sensory impaired students. They understood the concept and appreciated it.

We read these words of Carl Jung to the students:

Man feels himself isolated in the cosmos, because he is no longer involved with nature and has lost his emotional "unconscious" identity with natural phenomena.[12]

Liz Walker was extremely skillful in the translation for sign interpretations and converted the preceding quote into the following signed translation.

Now we don't live with animals. We don't live in the woods, therefore we forget about nature. This makes us feel alone, not related to nature.

One of the goals of this program was to cut through the emptiness of modern isolation through folk tales and nature to free the primal spirit, and in the process break the isolation of deafness as well.

Language arts teacher, Liz Walker, as well as social studies interpreter aide, Midge McGraw, saw and made note of positive attitudinal changes in students as a direct result of this program, although no actual scientific study was made.

This program was sponsored by the New Castle County Department of Parks and Recreation with funds from the Special Populations Section in connection with the 1981 International Year of the Disabled Person, through Recreational Specialist Carol Barnet.

Footnotes

[1]Jamake Highwater was keynote speaker at the Art Educators of New Jersey Convention, Cherry Hill, N.J. Information paraphrased from notes taken by Judith Schwab.

[2]Joseph L. Henderson, *Man and His Symbols, part II, Ancient Myths and Modern Man* (New York: Dell), p. 97.

[3]Jamake Highwater, *The Primal Mind* (New York: Harper and Row, 1981), p. 6.

[4]Paraphrase from Highwater lecture notes.

[5]*The Primal Mind*, p. 6.

[6]*Sensory Integration Special Interest Newsletter*, Vol. V, No. 2, 1982. American Occupational Therapy Association, 1383 Rice and Drive Sts., Rockville, MD 20850.

[7]Norman Feder, **American Indian Art** (New York: Abrams, 1971), p. 20.

[8]Cottie Arthur Burland, *North American Indian Mythology* (Feltham, England: Hamlyn-American, 1968), p. 12.

[9]Clare Lee Tammer, ed., *Indian Arts and Crafts* (Phoenix, Arizona Highways), p. 71. (2039 W. Lewis Ave., Phoenix, AZ 85009)

[10]Puppet purchased from Puppetry Store, Puppeteers of America, International Puppetry Convention, Washington, D.C.

[11]Paraphrase from Highwater lecture notes.

[12]Carl G. Jung, ed., *Man and His Symbols* (New York: Dell).

To Make String Puppet.

Materials: 2½-3 inch diameter styrofoam ball; four styrofoam cups; tissue paper; stiff wire; cardboard or ice cream spoons; felt and fabric; button and fishing line.

Construction:

The Head

For basic head, use one styrofoam ball cut in half. (Using a half cuts cost and provides a flat surface on which to work.)

Have children choose colored tissue paper from among assorted strong colors (no pastels). Using vivid colors to cover the face makes the effect more dramatic. Colors such as red, shocking pink, purple, brown, black, green, navy, bright blue are good offers. Only one color per head should be used.

Tear tissue paper into approximately ¾ x ¾ inch sizes and glue onto the styrofoam ball with a brush and diluted white glue. (Mix almost equal amount of water with glue.)

After the head is completely covered, begin building features (in a papier-mache, relief manner) using the same colored tissue, diluted glue and, when necessary, full strength glue to help features adhere. Noses, ears and lips can all be built onto the basic face in this way.

Cut white or off-white eye shapes from pieces of felt or other cloth and glue onto face area. After the glue dries, add buttons or sequins for the iris of the eyes.

The Body

Divide four styrofoam cups into two sets. Glue each set of cups together as shown (two cups can be used but is not as strong).

Decorate the outside of the cups with repeated patterns and designs such as a series of circles and triangles. Indelible marker pens, crayons, or cut pieces of felt and colored tissue all can be used to create exciting designs.

Cut out two cardboard arms or use ice cream spoons for arms. Puncture or drill a hole at one end of each arm. Puncture a hole on both sides of upper part of top cup. Insert a length of wire through cup and thread wire at each end through an arm hole. Bend ends of wire over to secure.

With a large weaving needle sew fishing line through styrofoam ball and cups as shown. Tie bottom of line to a button to secure. Leave extra length at top and tie a loop for a handle.

A simple skirt can be added to complete the puppet. To make skirt, cut out a 10 to 12 inch circle from fabric. The fabric can be any color or pattern; plaid, solid, dotted are all acceptable. A bamboo chalk or other compass is useful to measure and mark the circular skirt. Attach skirt to cup body by gluing to waist.

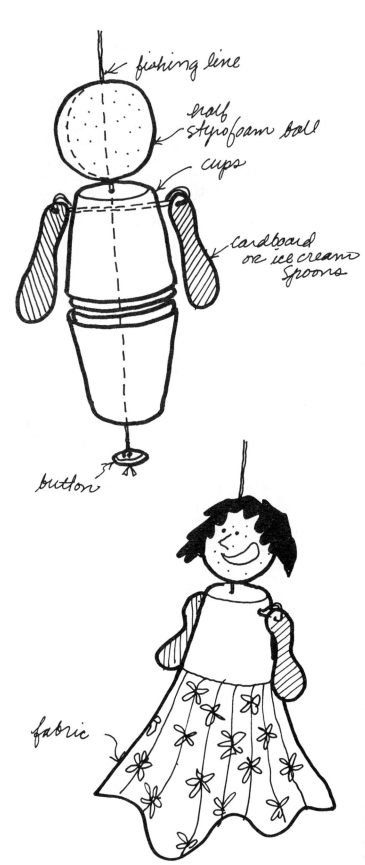

fishing line

half styrofoam ball

cups

cardboard or ice cream spoons

button

fabric

Kachina String Puppets—*Photo by Jamie Winder*

Eagle Rod Puppet soars in front of a screen for a presentation of "The Eagle and the Rock"—*Photo by Jamie Winder*

Building Vocabulary by Telling a Tale

By Judith Schwab

Deafness isolates the individual. Consequently classroom activities for the deaf student should focus on language development. Ideas cannot be exchanged without having language patterns to convey these ideas. Deaf students do not learn the patterns of meaningful communication without motivation.[1]

—Lee C. Murphy

We met the challenge of providing motivation by using puppetry as a nonverbal way to act out a fable. Hearing impaired high school students' senses were stimulated by a multimedia creative arts experience. The goal was to provide motivation to make students remember vocabulary words far above their third grade reading level. Presenting a vocabulary list to be memorized can be stifling to deaf students because studying a list is dry and uninteresting for those who struggle with language. However, present these same words in beautifully written prose through a multimedia experience and you have stimulated the imagination, piqued interest and developed a sense of personal involvement.

This type of experience, was given to high school students at the Margaret S. Sterck School for the Hearing Impaired in Newark, Delaware. As a visiting artist, I was able to arrange for author Dr. Jim Durkin to visit the Advanced II Literature Class with whom I had been working under the auspices of the New Castle County Department of Parks and Recreation, Special Populations Section in Northern Delaware. Durkin wrote a fable called "The Eagle and the Rock," which I believed could provide motivation for learning. Following is Dr. Durkin's description of the tale.

The Eagle and the Rock is a fable or folk tale about two main characters, each of whom has taken a definite position in life. One gets out and does, and the other just sits and indulges in pure being. They meet and, as Yin/Yang opposites, find themselves mightily attracted to each other. They embark together on a path through life which at first seems ideal; as a result of the blindness of both, due to the lack of wholeness in each, they meet with disaster. But in the wisdom of the TAO, that for which there is no opposite, the very characteristics which they valued least in themselves, that which was latent in them to make them each whole, turned disaster into a miracle which served to overcome the disintegrative forces of death.[2]

I realized that preparation for this kind of material had coincidently begun six months earlier with our focus on the values of Native American Culture through the study of folk tales. I refer the reader to the article in this section on "Native American Culture For Hearing Impaired." After Language Arts teacher Liz Walker read "The Eagle and the Rock," she too saw it as motivational prose. Walker feels that challenging material such as this must be presented to hearing impaired high school students because

Language used with hearing impaired students is often watered-down to make communication more efficient. A steady diet of such language results in an impoverished store of language from which students must draw. Exposure to more sophisticated language in construction and vocabulary not only gives more choices for later usage but also gives the student experience using contextual clues and grasping cognitive meaning.

Being a puppeteer and a painter, it was not surprising that I responded to the fable by picturing a rod puppet eagle flying into a watercolored landscape. In my mind's ear, I imagined the sounds I had heard on a record "Callings,"[3] and so I integrated "Lullaby From the Great Mother Whale for the Baby Seal Pups" from this recording with the visual images created by the students.

There were only three days remaining in my contract at the Margaret Sterck School when I began work on this project. Due to the lack of time, I completed some of the art work which normally could be accomplished by the students, i.e. creating landscape watercolors, taking slides of the watercolors, and building the core and frame of rod-puppets using a 2-liter plastic soda bottle body and wire wings. This prepared core was taken to class to be decorated and completed by the students.

In future puppet projects, everything from the painting of landscapes, photography, and puppet-making details could be done entirely by the students through their art, photography and language arts classes. Similar activities could also be incorporated into a science, social studies, and physical education program. For example:

Science	• *Study the geology of an area described in the tale.*
	• *Study the habits and habitat of eagles.*
	• *Design a mechanically balanced puppet.*
Social Studies	• *Study maps and landscapes of areas described in the fable.*
	• *Explore values highlighted by tale.*
Language Arts	• *Reinforce grammatical skills.*
	• *Build new vocabulary.*
	• *Develop skills needed to put on a show.*
Art	• *Do photography for slides.*
	• *Create puppets.*
	• *Paint watercolor landscapes.*
Physical Education	• *Develop large motor skills.*
	• *Encourage strength and coordination needed in working a large puppet.*

Preparing for the Tale

Prior to Dr. Durkin's visit, Liz Walker had her students read the folk tale. The students each received a personal copy of the tale. They were encouraged to guess at the meanings of long and formidable words such as *metamorphosis*. As the teacher signed the story, the students located each word or groups of words in phrases on their copies. They did this during the days when I was working elsewhere. Through this experience, the "students became aware," says teacher Liz Walker, "of synonyms, used in context, to help understand unknown words." On my next classroom visit, the eight students in the Advanced II Class became involved as a group in the surface sculpture and decoration of the prepared eagle rod-puppet. Some research photos of eagles in a variety of environments were brought to class by students. Some students

made tail feathers with construction paper while others worked on attaching the feathers to the wings. Others decorated the body, while still others sculpted the head. The creation of the Eagle required two class periods.

In preparation for our final class meeting, Ms. Walker prepared a 24 inch x 36 inch newsprint set of visuals, on which she lettered parts of the fable with 2 inch high letters. In this way, she could reinforce the vocabulary in "The Eagle and the Rock" before our guest, Dr. Jim Durkin, read the tale.

During the presentation, Ms. Walker wore a microphone that was connected to hearing aids the students wore. She pointed to a particular phrase on the sheets with one hand, as she signed with the other. She also spoke and interpreted and asked questions.

What was your latest achievement of pleasure?

What does the eagle do for a livelihood?

Students answered signing, "Eagle is persistent in working," and "The eagle is constant in pursuit of goals."

In this way, Ms. Walker pulled meaning and interpretation from the group before beginning with the aesthetic aspects of the program. Once satisfied with student comprehension of the material, she introduced Dr. Durkin, and then she sat next to him, signing his words, to ensure a total communication experience. The students watched while Durkin drew a tiny pair of glasses out of his pocket. He unfolded them once, then doubled their size once again, and like magic, they grew.

As he prepared our group to experience his tale, he told us that he was sharing a recurring dream, one that he had had so many nights that he finally put pen to paper and recorded it. He told students that he had made many drafts of the story before he was satisfied with it, and, in fact, even changed some words in the reading of the tale. Students were surprised and impressed with the fact that revision was necessary. They thought an established author did not have to go through such a laborious, trial and error process. A student signed, "You mean when you first write it down, it's not the way you want it?" The idea that Durkin spends hundreds of hours refining his work gave these students courage to struggle with their own writing.

Durkin discussed with the students some of the meanings and illusions depicted in his prose. He also helped them relate many of the emotions to their own lives. He explained that the story was comprised of two real things, an eagle and a rock, but the entire story was imagined. He asked, "Do you ever dream? Do you ever daydream?" The tale began, with students at rapt attention, completely caught up in the magic of the moment. As Durkin mentioned the rock in the story, he took a small speckled stone from his pocket and handed it to the student closest to him. The student examined the stone and passed it to his next closest classmate to see and touch, as he had done as the story was told.

The Eagle and the Rock

The Pleasure of Achievement and the Achievement of Pleasure

By Jim Durkin

Once, not long ago, an eagle could be seen soaring high in the sky on its way to the achievement of tasks it performed to fulfill its livelihood. It was inspiring to watch this great gray bird silhouetted against the heavens, carving its eager wings through the clear thin air and shoving it energetically behind. Summer, Winter, Spring and Fall did this persistent creature ply the sky in quest of its goals and dreams. And the land lay far below.

One day, close to noon, this dedicated soul was winging its way over a place in the Northern Country they called Old Woman's Bay. Suddenly its sharp eyes discerned something far below, something lying just at the boundary between the water and the land. It was only a rock, a rock that by all rights should not have been singled out from its millions strewn like stars, patternlessly across the land. Nevertheless, the flying arrow of the eagle's acute perception cleaved through the ether and envisioned this particular rock. This rock, and this rock alone shone out like a beacon for the eagle and stirred up deep feelings within its heart. Nothing like this had ever happened before. Never before had the eagle experienced such surging, paining intensity pumping so fearfully within its breast.

Though seldom deterred from its unwavering path of achievement, the eagle, arrested by the sight of the rock, seemed to decompose in midflight. It was like the moment the gunfighter experiences just after the bullet with his name on it penetrates his body, and just before he falls. But while the shot gunfighter falls, the eagle gathered itself together in an instant and veered sharply but smoothly

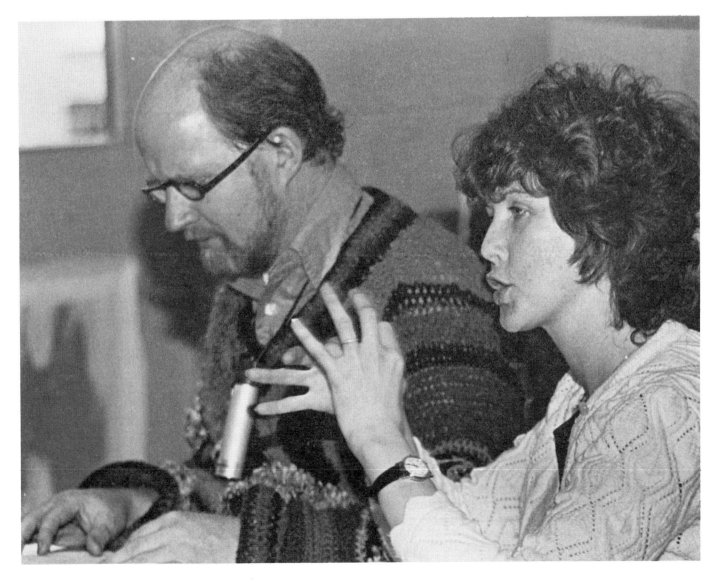

Jim Durkin shares his recurring dream with students while Liz Walker sings—*Photo by Jamie Winder*

downward and leftward toward its stone. In graceful ever narrowing curves the eagle approached the shoreline. It clamped down its wing and tail feathers to brake against the air and its velocity vanished. It alighted next to the spot of the rock on the shore of Old Woman's Bay.

The rock was not so large, extending ten centimeters at most along its length and six centimeters at most along its width. Its general shape was that of a shallow double angle, bending along both its length and width. It was blunted, even concave, at the front and rounded at the rear. If the rock were seen swimming it would give the appearance of a decapitated seal veering upwards and rightwards through the water.

The color of the eagle's rock was a dull salmon pink, although its surface was somewhat mottled with whitish flecks, silvery flecks, and a few translucent shiny flecks. Geometrically, the rock had a structure with seven facets, although the edges of these facets had long since been rounded off by time. The largest and flattest facet was brushed with a thin ivory colored coating which looked like it had been painted on. It was on this plane that the rock had let itself come to rest long before on the shore of Old Woman's Bay.

The eagle gently cupped the rock in its talons and beat its wings again. The rock offered no resistance and the pair of them rose up. A joyous excitement welled up within the rock as they rapidly gained altitude. After being wedged in with all the others for so long, the wide perspective on the world they achieved filled the rock with pleasurable excitement. It was exhilarated by the rush of cool air hissing past them as it nestled securely within the eagle's tender tenure. At the same time the great eagle began to experience an immense pleasure from the new partnership. It began to take exalted pride in its stewardship of the rock. It altered its travel plans to cover the maximally scenic route; it took care to protect its rock from undue ravages of the elements; it strove to be most attentive to any and all of the rock's personal wishes.

The arrangement seemed perfect as the couple flew through the Fall and Winter seasons. The rock, who had always been oriented toward pleasure as it lounged below in the warmth of the daily sun, now achieved supernal happiness as it surveyed beautiful vistas from on high. The eagle, who had always been oriented toward achievement as it busily ran its endless errands, pleasured itself immeasurably by providing for its rock's every need and joy. Truly, the pair of them had developed a completely harmonious relationship.

Although attempts at scientific speculation such as this are often idle, one cannot but be tempted to conjecture that it was the increased level of cosmic radiation they encountered at such high altitudes that was responsible for generating the change that gradually took place in the rock. Neither of them noticed the change at first because the rate of change was so slight. But as the metamorphosis accelerated and its results became indubitably palpable, it was their willing blindness that prevented them from doing something about it in time.

The rock was growing. It had become pregnant with life. But the eagle was too engrossed in the pleasure of achievement and the rock too involved in the achievement of

pleasure to attend seriously to what was happening. And so the once fortuitous partnership persisted on into the Winter months as if the situation had not altered at all. The eagle simply pumped out higher levels of energy in order maintain the same altitudes and velocities as before on its round around the sky. In fact, the increasing effort was experienced as an invigorating challenge. As for the rock, the increased wind resistance and attendant turbulence as well as the heightened effects of its own inertia stimulated even greater sensations of pleasure. And so they went on, heedlessly, fecklessly.

The catastrophe came just as they were striving to surmount a snow capped ridge to reach a peaceful valley beyond. The end was sudden. Just at the summit of the ridge, the eagle's great heart simply burst asunder. The rock had completely rounded out by now and had achieved a weight of several kilos, almost as much as the eagle had weighed. After the death, the eagle and the rock plummeted down together and hit the snow just over the peak of the ridge. The eagle, even in death, did not forsake its responsibility to the rock, for its caressing talons, still protecting its treasure, cushioned the impact upon the now fragile sphere.

The couple lay still together as the biting Winter wind swirled relentlessly and uncaringly around them. The once-great bird was now nothing but a frozen carcass, and the rock now nothing but an interloper displaced far from its shoreline home. As the savage wind persisted, it was only the insulation provided by the soft down and feathers of the eagle's corpse that enabled the spark of life that had generated itself within the rock to persist through the long Winter season. But miraculously, the spark of life did indeed persist, and when the intensisty of the Spring sun's warmth had waxed sufficiently, the process that had begun in the Fall brought itself to fruition. One bright day, seven lustly little ones struggled out of the living egg, slithered playfully, if unskillfully, down the slope of the ridge to the grassy plains below, thus engendering a new race of creatures for the world.

Summary of Project

Ms. Walker gave her reaction to the project by saying,

The benefits of an integrated multimedia program such as this in allowing students to handle words much above their supposed third grade reading level are three fold. One is in giving experience with words that challenge their ability to understand context, although they may not take from the fable what an adult may, they will begin to use the same skills of educatedly filling in the blanks. Also, being exposed to beautifully written prose and artfully rendered imagination may subtly affect their own writing. Finally, meeting an established author gives them encouragement they need in their writing careers.

We also briefly discussed the universality of nonverbal symbols. Durkin spoke about the way one group can own arbitrary things such as language. Walker responded that "the deaf do not own the language. It is as if they are only renting the words." We agreed that visual, nonverbal symbols such as puppets and pictures provide a universal language that can cut through many barriers to communication. Durkin said, "When you live in a verbal universe, the words can deplete you."

This supports my feeling about motivating expression and cognitive growth with creative and visual arts such as puppetry and music. When art provides aesthetic experience, learning is stimulated as students use new modes of expression. The effect manifests itself in the high level of enthusiasm I see generated by students involved in creative arts experience.

Since many of the students involved in this program were reassigned to other literature teachers when they reentered school in September, it was difficult to evaluate retention and carry over of the project. However, one student Jeffrey, was assigned to Liz Walker's English class again.

When all of Ms. Walker's students were told to bring one new vocabulary word to class each week, Jeffrey brought the word "less heedly." Ms. Walker signed, "No such word." Jeffrey signed, "Yes, it means not care, from Eagle and Rock story." Liz Walker took out her copy of the tale. Jeffrey pointed to the word heedlessly. Ms. Walker signed "Yes, but see, Jeff, 'heed' is always the first syllable in this word." "Heedlessly," Jeff signed, "yes, like carelessly." Ms. Walker felt that this was powerful proof that there was cognitive retention over the summer break from a motivational creative arts experience which took place in the spring.

Adapting the Tale to Elementary Students

The previously described project "Building Vocabulary" was used a second time at Sterck School with students doing all the work and culminating in an all school assembly program.

In addition to the students in Liz Walker's language class, other students became involved in acting out the story with nonverbal body movement to explore alternate ways of communicating the same information.

An adaptation of the tale was prepared for the elementary children. This shortened story enabled teachers to prepare young students to understand and appreciate the assembly program.

The speech pathologist worked with the students

who verbalized the shortened tale and the audiologist experimented with the sound. She had students wear their FM units and a tape of the music "Callings" was played directly into the hearing aids. In addition, the sound was broadcast for the audience that did not wear the units.

The construction, performance and projection of the puppet show was similar to that done for the upper level presentation. However, because of the time allotment more students were actively involved. Students were able to prepare all of the art work themselves and develop the dramatic aspects. These dramatic additions were exciting interpretive movements which were designed fully by the students and highlighted the show.

The overall effect of the performance was heightened by a spotlight which gave enough light for the audience to see the action of the tale and threw shadows on the walls as the students moved about. (The lighting gave the performers a cloak of darkness in which they could move more freely.)

As the performance began, eight students participated as eagles, gliding with their arms positioned as wings. Then, half of the group became rocks, moving just in front of their eagle partners which gave the appearance of their being carried. As each eagle strained to fly higher, the student's face and body reflected the effort. Students dropped to the ground as the eagle's heart collapsed from the weight.

With arms raised, all particpants then became the cold winter wind and they repeatedly leaned from east to west. Spring was signified by students positioning themselves with arms touching each other's shoulders, heads down, feet spread apart. In the shell like position of the egg, they gently rocked from side to side. Next they became the new life within the egg. Using short choppy movements, they seemed to break out of the shell. Finally, students built up the movements of being lusty by jumping happily in the air. They entered the world by hopping off out of sight.

Both the high school and elementary level performances emphasized that there are many ways in which to communicate. The hearing-impaired child needs constantly to be reminded of alternate methods and encouraged to assimilate new techniques.

One of the comments made during the project by Language Arts teacher Barb Hobart on abstract concepts made impact.

The kids didn't understand as much as we did (how an eagle could mate with a rock). But this experience was a start toward understanding the abstractions we deal with in our lives. I do believe that the students understood the relationship between the eagle and the rock. They enjoyed seeing the shadow of the eagle flying across the landscape. They were fascinated by the slide projection: It was not quite a motion picture, but gave the feeling of movement because of the moving puppet and the changing landscapes.

The following photographs document the project in action as done for the elementary students.

Students portraying the cold winter wind—*Photo by Jamie Winder*

The Seven Lusty, Little Ones are shown in shadow—*Photo by Jamie Winder*

Synopsis of "The Eagle and the Rock"

By Dr. Jim Durkin.

(Adapted for use with elementary pupils by Judith Schwab, Liz Walker, Ann Merrill)

The eagle is a powerful bird. He flies high in the sky searching for food.

One day he sees a rock lying happily on the soft sand, warmed by the gentle waves.

The eagle wants the rock. He picks up the rock and carries it through the sky. The rock enjoys being taken care of by the eagle. The eagle loves showing the rock his view of the earth.

Neither the eagle nor the rock realize something is changing. The rock is growing into an egg. Now the rock/egg is pregnant with life. She enjoys watching the earth, cradled by the eagle's strong talons.

Seasons change; spring, summer, fall, and winter. Winter snows cover the mountain tops.

The eagle tries to fly high but the rock/egg is so heavy with new life that it is a big effort. The eagle's heart cannot work any longer. His heart bursts.

The eagle falls dead onto the mountain but his feathers cushion the rock/egg's fall so its shell does not break. His feathers warm the rock/egg.

In the spring the rock/egg breaks open and seven babies are born. The "seven lusty, little ones" enter the world.

126

The finale—*Photo by Jamie Winder*

Related Activities

The Puppet Biography that follows provides an excellent opportunity to stimulate imagination and reinforce language arts' skills. As students complete this outline, they can be encouraged to use new and varied vocabulary. The format helps students to use logical order and to express ideas in complete sentences.

An abbreviated version of the story was used prior to the assembly program and the Puppet Biography was used after the puppet production to help students verbalize the characters they wished to build into the story line. After the production, the Biography can provide a review of the elements or be a springboard for creative writing and dramatics experiences.

- **Puppet Biography**

Puppet's Name: *Super Joey, the Eagle*

Puppet's Address: *Mountain Drive, P.O. Box Route 8, Dublin, Ireland 19019*

Puppet's Appearance:
 Color of hair *Black*
 Color of eyes *Blue*
 Color of skin *Black*

Puppet's Picture: (Leave space for drawing.)

Puppet's Activities: (Students complete sentences)
 Puppet loves to *fly and eat and he loves to help his friends.*
 Puppet is *afraid of monsters and hates stinky tails.*
 Puppet hates to *kill his friends.*
 Puppet never *gets to buy food.*
 Puppet eats *pizza and noodles.*
 Puppet sleeps *at night in a bat cave.*
 Puppet's friends are *the bats and eagles.*
 You can add more things yourself: *My puppet's birthday is December 100.*

Acknowledgments

I wish to thank the art, science and social studies teachers as well as the support staff—the speech therapists, the shop and office personnel—for their cooperation and support. Some supplied materials, others gave extra classroom time. I extend a special acknowledgment to Principal Sue Lee who urged me before I began working at their school to find a way whenever possible to include music in my programs. She felt that it was important for Sterck hearing impaired students to experience music as an enrichment, of which they are often bereft.

Two outsiders also contributed to the project— Jamie Winder Photography of Newark, Delaware, and Sherri Goodill, movement therapist from the Terry Center in Wilmington, Delaware.

Lastly, I thank Liz Walker and Dr. Jim Durkin without whose wholehearted contributions this program would not have been successful. A special thanks also to Dr. Durkin for allowing us permission to reprint his tale.

To Make Eagle Rod Puppet

Materials: Quart size plastic soda bottle; four-foot long 3/4-inch wood dowel; thumbtack; soft, thick aluminum wire (hardware store); oak tag paper; and brown tissue paper.

Construction: *To prepare rod*—Puncture a 3/4-inch hole in center of bottle laying in horizontal position as shown. Slip dowel up inside bottle body entirely. Push thumbtack through opposite side of bottle into end of dowel to hold down in place.

To create wing frame and talons—Bend aluminum wire first into one wing shape. Wrap wire around bottle a few times, then bring wire to bottom of bottle body and bend wire into two talon shapes. Then bring wire back up and form another wing shape on opposite side of bottle. Wrapping wire again around bottle a few times and snip off. Cover top and bottom of each wing frame with a matching shape cut from oak tag paper and tape or glue in place over frames (remember eagles have especially long wing spans).

Add an oak tag head and beak profile on both sides of neck end of bottle. Decorate eagle with fringed tissue paper for a feathery look.

To make expanding rock—Tape a length of tubing along length of dowel with balloon taped to end of tubing arranged near talons. A bulldog clip can be used on tubing to pinch off air from balloon when not in use.

Footnotes

[1] Lee C. Murphy, "Video Tape as a Motivator for Nonhearing Students, *Teaching Exceptional Children*, vol. X (1974), p. 10.

[2] James Durkin, Ph.D., wrote this tale expressly for the Sterck School project and has given his permission for it to be published in this book.

[3] Paul Winter Consort, *Callings*, "Lullaby from the Great Mother Whale for the Baby Seal Pups," Living Music Records.

127

SPECIAL WORKS BY THEATER TROUPES
The Hutchinson Sunflower Puppeteers
Director Claudia Leonesio Article by Repha Buckman

The Underground Railway
Directors Debra Wise, Jown Lewandowski and Wes Sanders
Article by Edward Pazzanese and Debra Wise

Claudia Leonesio leads a discussion with troupe members. They grew through the time spent together and all became very conscious of the closeness that had developed within the troupe—*Photo by Tom Bell*

The Hutchinson Sunflower Puppeteers

The Work of Claudia Leonesio
By Repha Buckman

They said it could never be done, that the handicapped could not perform well enough nor would they have the stamina to tour. And they were wrong. A two year puppetry program in Hutchinson, Kansas gave a group of developmentally disabled adults the opportunity to present dozens of performances to hundreds of people in Kansas, Nebraska and finally Georgia.

As I worked with this project, I was reminded of my childhood, growing up in a valley full of rivers and walnut trees filled with houses and people. Above this valley rose two hills; one was known as College Hill. The marble steps to its stately brick buildings on this college campus were worn with the footsteps of students climbing to the stars. Further out, beyond the edge of town, rose Third Hill, as we called it, or the State Training School. Housed there were handicapped adults. However, their chronological age meant nothing, for regardless of age, they were lost in childhood, captured by physical, emotional and mental handicaps in a world which could offer little outside of shelter and food. Their days were filled for them, and the walks to their limestone buildings were worn with footsteps that shuffled across red brick with small aspirations in contrast to College Hill.

It was a revelation to see the Sunflower Puppeteers go beyond the limitations of a Third Hill and move into experiences which gave them the opportunity to display their special talents. The project began in 1980 when Les Benefil, Director of Recreational Services for the Handicapped, Inc. of the Hutchinson, Kansas Recreation Commission envisioned a performing arts program which would offer cultural enrichment for the handicapped. Two factors influenced him to try the medium of puppetry. First, in college he had been introduced to puppetry as a therapeutic aid in working with the handicapped. Second, the adults served by the Hutchinson Recreation Commission had markedly diverse disability areas; while some could not articulate, others had restricted mobility. Puppetry as an art form could easily allow a performing arts experience for everyone, even those who did not have the ability to speak or to move freely. Claudia Leonesio was hired to set up this new program. It became her primary task to implement classes in puppetry and help carry out the vision of a group of touring puppeteers composed of adult handicapped performers. The most important aspect of this program was that the handicapped adult have an opportunity to perform. Regardless of the severity of the disability, everyone who participated and learned, would experience performance in front of an audience and also be part of the touring group. Everyone would be a star. It was a lofty aspiration.

In order to meet and establish preliminary relationships with potential puppeteers, Leonesio worked with the existing Kansas Coffee Houses, which were sponsored by the Kansas Arts Commission and the Association for Retarded Citizens and conducted by Hutchinson Recreation Commission. These projects provided exposure to the performing arts for the professional as well as the amateur, the handicapped as well as the nonhandicapped. In addition, the Coffee Houses served as a social normalization vehicle to mainstream audiences.

After several months of observations and casual conversations at the Coffee Houses, Leonesio had established the preliminary relationships and was ready to begin the puppetry class. Sessions were to be held weekly and were scheduled for evenings to make the time convenient for the largest number of people. The classes would meet at the Hutchinson Repertory Theatre which provided a theatrical environment.

Beginning Sessions

For the first puppetry session, the chairs had been arranged in a large semicircle. The room was flooded with light and an assortment of ready made mouth, hand and rod puppets were accessible and obvious in the room.

When the puppeteers arrived they were greeted and allowed time to acclimate and discuss small events of the day. As soon as their eyes began to wander to the puppets, Leonesio took the opportunity to encourage a hands-on experience with the puppets. Once they had warmed up, they began trying on various puppets and establishing puppet friendships which would last over the months.

After the introductory session, the next several classes were devoted to exercises which provided the dexterity skills necessary to manipulate the puppets. For instance, the puppeteers sat in a semicircle, arms outstretched and palms flat. Following the leader's instructions, the group would move their thumbs alternately, toward and away from their palms. (This was the basic movement needed to open and close a puppet's mouth.) It was important for disabled puppeteers to build up their muscles and strengthen weak fingers and arms.

After this initial skill was mastered, the group spent time working with the puppet characters in learning to synchronize movement with sound. This was done through a song activity. By themselves or in groups of varying sizes, class members stood behind the bare plastic pipe framework of their not yet complete puppet stage, moving to the sounds of recorded country and rock music. They practiced the same song over and over until it was memorized as puppets energetically moved mouths and bodies or danced, trying to coordinate with the music. In spite of concentrated effort, it was not a task easily conquered by these disabled puppeteers.

After weeks of frustrating practice, one of the puppeteers and his bird puppet challenged the group to progress. During a session in which puppets' mouths flapped in disharmony, Bill's bird twisted and jerked into the air and in sudden exasperation Bill had his bird call out, "These dumbies will never get it!" Everyone stood stunned, looking at this small bird and his puppeteer. Bill's cerebral palsied body shook and strained as he determinedly manuevered his puppet's mouth in perfect timing with the music. No one spoke.

The rest knew that their practice was being put to the test. They had to show Bill that they could likewise move their puppets' mouths *only* when the words were sung. Following Bill's lead, a jumble of characters—pirate, frog, alligator, snake, flower and monkey—began to move their mouths in perfect timing with the words of the song. Another milestone on the difficult road had been met.

Advanced Sessions

Having developed some basic skills, the puppeteers began a new series of classes. They were to use a pretaped script and a full stage. Their first performance piece was a medieval puppet script call *Sir Eglamore and the Dragon* by Lisl Behr. Some of the initial mouth and rod practice puppets were spruced up in new costumes of velvet and satin, edged with gold and these, along with some newly created puppets made by outside volunteers, seemed splendid to the puppeteers who were to be cast in the play.

Puppets were matched with disabilities. The part of the irate father in the play was given to a man with cerebral palsy who could hardly control his convulsive hand movements. The puppet appropriately quaked with anger during the performance. The puppeteer's own disability enhanced his characterization of the role. A blind, mentally disabled man played Sir Eglamore's horse. The puppet was designed so that one hand fit into the mouth of the horse and the other hand operated a rod connected to the horse's rear. The particular design enabled the puppeteer to know the exact position of his puppet at all times and he was delighted with his ability to make it gallop.

One of the most constructive aspects of the project was the group learning to assemble the stage as a team and take it apart. It was an important part of the training for touring. At every opportunity, proper techniques and care of equipment were stressed. The group labored over the many different sections of the complex stage. At first it took much of the class time just to set up or strike it down, but eventually they learned what pieces went where and who was responsible for various chores. When the puppeteers adjourned each session, it was a regular requirement that the rods were properly packed in canvas bags, the puppets in trunks, the curtains folded and the stage disassembled and put away.

Motivating the Group

As she developed rapport with the puppeteers, Leonesio was able to overcome many of the puppeteer's individual fears and frustrations. Her standard motivation and control throughout the entire project was praise. "You have worked so hard and I am proud of you. Don't give up now. You're doing very well," she would constantly encourage them.

In order to focus the class, Leonesio used meditation exercises to open each session. Setting the mood and atmosphere for the rest of the sessions, these calming moments allowed the puppeteers to put aside the cares, worries and concerns of the day and arise refreshed to greet their puppets.

The meditation exercises were followed by concentration, hand, and shoulder exercises. This ritual of preparation focused energies and lengthened attention spans. Through the repetition of individual puppet movements, the development of emotional expression, and dialogue and movement improvisations, the seeds of characterization were planted. Developing technique and performance abilities was a long, slow process. This was augmented by seeing films and live theatre and learning to discern a good performance from a mediocre one. To help discourage frustration, each class ended with a completely improvised puppet dance by each puppeteer to a popular recording, followed with a bow. As each puppeteer began to know the hand and rod puppets, inhibitions decreased and individual creativity emerged. They had discovered a new method of communication.

It was discovered that in addition to being a performance medium, the puppets allowed interaction among the puppeteers that was less threatening than standard socialization activities. As the class perceived each other's physical and emotional difficulties, they learned the cause and effect of their actions and how the process influenced individuals, as well as the group. They grew through the time spent together and all became very conscious of the closeness that had developed within the group. The puppeteers were also very protective of each other and helpful as well. They felt almost ready for their first performance but they still needed one thing— a name.

The Hutchinson Sunflower Puppeteers

There might have been many names chosen for the puppeteers, all equally descriptive and suitable, but they were called The Hutchinson Sunflower Puppeteers. The use of Hutchinson gave identity to the group since this was their home base. In addition, "Sunflower" is significant because it is the state flower of Kansas, and it is also a flower which follows the sun. The sunflower symbolizes that the disabled are here on earth to give and receive love much as the sunflower gives and receives the warmth of the sun— unconditionally.

Now that they had a name, a performance was arranged at Dillion Outdoor Educational Center and the puppeteers were ready. While practice made them confident, they were buoyed also by their recent sacrifices for this privilege. On opening night, they learned that the performance made all practice and hard work worthwhile, their horizons were expanding outward. Individual improvement had been vast. The troupe had earned the right to perform at the Hutchinson Recreation Center Coffee Houses and to travel throughout the state in the fall.

As if to reinforce their accomplishment, another performance opportunity presented itself locally. *Sir Eglamore* fit beautifully at the Hutchinson Public Library's Medieval Outdoor Faire. And there, training was again put to the test as a heavy rainstorm approached and Kansas winds whipped and tore at the stage, loosening its structure. Puppeteers, instead of being discouraged, grabbed the stage to stabilize it and puppets went right on performing. Even the horse bobbed agitatedly and the smile on puppeteer

Performing "The Blue Willow" with Bunraku style puppets—*Photo by Les Benefil*

Steve's face said it all. Although unable to see and severely mentally handicapped, he stood and with no assistance, moved the horse on a wooden stick, up and down. The fact that the performance ended before the rains poured down was secondary to the thrill of seeing Steve respond so positively.

The time had come to add another show to the repertoire and to experiment with style. *THE BLUE WILLOW*, written by Lewis Mahlman and David Cadwalader Jones, went into rehearsal and many new theatrical concepts were introduced. The puppeteers wore black robes and used body puppets in the style of Bunraku, a traditional Japanese art form using large scale puppets. All action took place in front of the stage from which the puppeteers made their entrances and exits. Prior to this, the stage manager could easily cue everyone backstage. They were now on their own. Only entrances could be cued. Retention levels were very low and, in addition, body movements and stage directions had to be learned. At this stage, instruction in mime was given to increase body awareness. This greatly enhanced manipulation of both the Bunraku and the hand style puppets. At the end of each rehearsal, each puppeteer was expected to offer comments, suggestions and positive criticism. This instilled an esprit de corps, pride in performance, and discouraged frustration. They persevered for the pure joy of performing.

The Traveling Troupe

The Sunflower Puppeteers were a success. Following the State Fair where they performed for seven hundred and fifty people, touring began in earnest. From Central Kansas to Western Kansas, the troupe moved and developed and learned more of their world as they gained an appreciation for the rigors of a life in touring theatre. In addition, everywhere they performed, they left behind new friends who felt richer for having met them.

As performers, artists and achievers, the Sunflower Puppeteers were ready for the Kansas Association for Retarded Citizens Performing Arts Competition held at Marymount College in Salina, Kansas. This was the culmination of one of the primary goals that recreational director Les Benefil and Claudia Leonesio had originally set. After a year and a half of preparation, the brightest moment came when the troupe picked up the event's first place drama award in competition with one hundred and ninety performers.

Following their rest after the competition, the puppeteers presented several shows in the Hutchinson area and then toured to Norfolk, Nebraska for A Very Special Arts Festival where they gave two performances. But their longest, most difficult tour lay ahead. And they had one month to get ready.

The Sunflower Puppeteers were honored to perform at the National Puppeteers of America Puppetry Festival in Atlanta, Georgia. Because of the length of the Festival performance scheduled, the puppeteers needed an additional script. A piece entitled *Sweet Unicorn* written by Repha Buckman and Claudia Leonesia was chosen and it was unlike anything the troupe had ever done, abstract and surrealistic. But from the first playing of the pre-recorded tape, the puppeteers delighted in the enchanting fairy and unicorn characters in the story.

The troupe left for Atlanta still practicing *The Blue Willow* and *Sweet Unicorn*. As the plains and hills of Kansas and Missouri fell behind, the tape played frequently in the travelling van and continued on through Kentucky, Tennessee and Georgia. When the troupe had arrived at their destination it did not disappoint them. Huge magnolia trees lined the pool where they were staying. Fragrant blossoms hung heavy as the puppeteers climbed to their rooms to sleep. And in his slumber, David cried out for all of the troupe, "Atlanta, Georgia! I finally made it!" It was a long term goal and a busy time for in addition to the Puppetry Festival performance, Special Audience's Inc. booked five performances in the greater Atlanta area which defrayed the troupe's travel expenses.

The troupe had spent ten physically grueling days on the road and weathered it like troupers. They had brought laughter and light and the gift of puppetry to hundreds of people.

Summary of Project

The puppeteers had shown that the developmentally disabled do have special talents. Those talents only need direction and guidance. To improve performance skills, Leonesio continued to evaluate each show with troupe members and reinforce skills through constructive repetition of comments. This assessment was important to the growth of the troupe because as Leonesio expressed, "It was not important that they were disabled, but it was important to seek improvement and fair analysis of performance."

Through my time with the Sunflower Puppeteers, I met and came to respect many people, some handicapped, some nonhandicapped. Some of them shared their goals and dreams with me. At one time, not too long ago, it would have been difficult to find a place where a touring puppet company such as this one composed of disabled adults could experience

A troupe member reaches out and shares a puppet with the audience—*Photo by Repha Buckman*

their own uniqueness, reflected in the faces and applause of audiences. Puppets offered a fine opportunity to extend the boundaries of not only the puppeteers, but also of those they touched.

The introduction of puppets not only implemented a creative learning experience, but also had far deeper consequences. It had an impact as a social instrument because those handicapped puppeteers with their perseverance and commitment have shown that the developmentally disabled can not only manage and perform with puppets as a troupe, and do them well, but they can also withstand the rigors of touring with professionalism and pride in themselves.

There are still institutions like Third Hill that house adult handicapped. And there are hundreds more disabled living in halfway houses or at home who will be chained to non-productive lives if allowed. However, if as adults they can be repeatedly exposed to a flow of ideas and creativity, they will strive for the stars, to shine with them when the show ends and the applause begins. All they need is a chance.

CREDITS:

The Hutchinson Sunflower Puppeteers are produced by Recreation Services for the Handicapped, Inc., Les Benefil, Director, of the Hutchinson, Ks. Recreation Commission, Les Keller, Director with the cooperation and support of the Kansas Arts Commission, a state agency, and the National Endowment for the Arts, a federal agency. Marty Rothwell, the Kansas Association for Retarded Citizens and the Hutchinson Repertory Theatre were extremely instrumental in the growth and development of the troupe.

Repha Glenn Buckman, a former Kansas educator, served as business manager for the Hutchinson Repertory Theater. She is currently an Artist-in-Schools for the Wichita Public Schools and serves on the Kansas Arts Commission as a documentary writer. Her writing credits are numerous and include *Repha*, an album and *Cleaving the Surface* a portfolio collection. In 1976, she was selected to Outstanding Young Women in America. She is also a theatrical director and her show, MISHIMA, a Noh adaptation, won five special awards at the 1983 Festival of American Community Theaters in Kansas.

Claudia Carruth Leonesio founded, developed and served as Artistic Director of the Hutchinson Sunflower Puppeteers for two years. Currently she is the artistic director/owner of Chatterbox Puppets of California and is in the process of developing a handicapped awareness program. She has performed educational puppet shows throughout California and served as Special Projects Coordinator of the Hutchinson Repertory Theater. In 1981, she was selected to Outstanding Young Women of America and was awarded by the Association of Kansas Theater for exemplary work in theater with the handicapped. A graduate of the University of California at Santa Barbara, Ms. Leonesio received a UC President's Undergraduate Fellowship Award for her work with theater for young audiences.

Puppetry gave students an opportunity to experience the parts of themselves—creativity, spontaneity, playfulness—they thought that they had to bury in order to get along—*Photo by Lorenzo Deitch*

Building Self Esteem through Puppetry

A Residency at the Robert White School
By Ed Pazzanese and Debra Wise

Puppetry and drama are media which encourage children to take on roles and work through their own defenses. Combined, these vehicles provide an avenue which allows the children to express their own stories and concerns. This chapter describes a residency project developed by the Underground Railway Puppets and Actors Theater for special students at the Robert White School in Boston during the spring of 1983.

The Underground Railway Puppets and Actors Theater was founded in 1974 in Oberlin, Ohio and is currently based in Cambridge, Massachusetts. The company members were determined to bring their theater performances to a broad spectrum of people of all classes, rather than residing in a fixed place serving a more traditional theater-going audience. The company's members are Debra Wise, John Lewandowski and Wes Sanders.

The title, Underground Railway, signifies more than the mobility of the group. It was choosen to commemorate the historical Underground Railway, the network of secret hideouts and brave people that helped Black Americans escape the slavery in the south before and during the Civil War. Harriett Tubman, the Railroad's most famous "conductor," had the imagination to envision a better world, and the will to join with others to make that vision a reality for hundreds of people.

The members of this inventive performance troupe come from very different backgrounds, but share a desire to make theater that invites people to look at our world in a new way, to explore alternatives and to celebrate the hope, the spirit and the imagination that makes change possible. They draw their material from a variety of sources—history, culture, mythology, folklore, and social concerns. The company attempts to produce theater that responds to the needs of the various communities that make up its audience.

Through their educational residency programs, the company has learned to know its audience before beginning to work with them. In both school and community settings the theater plans jointly with the staff of the sponsoring organization to design a program that addresses the needs of the participants. Each population is unique, with special needs, gifts and opportunities.

At the Robert White School members of the Underground Railway met with social studies teacher Kathy Greeley and the school's art teacher, to discuss a residency program for students. This company was selected for the project because it was felt that the actors treated students with respect, responded to them as whole people and recognized the stressful patterns in their lives that provoked their behavioral difficulties.

Students at this school are twelve to twenty years old and have been asked to leave previously attended public schools because of their disruptive behavior. They are from economically disadvantaged neighborhoods and have been labeled emotionally disturbed. Most of the women students are mothers.

Many of these students have limited views of the world around them. During the Artist-in-Residence Program, it was observed that some students did not know that Boston is a city, or Massachusetts a state. One student from Charlestown had never left his neighborhood until he went to this school in downtown Boston. This program was in response to the need to increase the awareness of the students about life outside their own urban environment.

The young people at the Robert White School are struggling with the effects of extreme economic and cultural deprivation. All of the teens are poor and have been damaged by racism and isolated by inner-city life. Most come from troubled family backgrounds and have had early experiences with violence. The ill effects of parental stress have been handed down to the children. As a result of the environment and the attitudes it projects, the students suffer. The students have very low self-esteem and assume that they will fail at most tasks.

Consequently, the main educational goal of this residency was to help students value what they did so they would learn to more fully respect themselves and their work. The program was designed to increase the workshop participants' skills in articulating what they felt or saw and in communicating an emotional problem or idea. Through puppetry, the students developed communication and group interactive skills. Improvising with a puppet was a more comfortable way for teens to express their fears, dreams, hopes and aspirations.

The Program

The format of the program allowed the students to choose either puppetry or acting classes. It was realized early that some students would consider puppets "kid's stuff" and that those with low self-esteem might easily balk at the idea of making puppets. For those students, there was the acting class option and students who enrolled in that class were very eager to perform, to be actors or directors. There were other students, however, who didn't want anything to do with acting. These students felt much more comfortable making a character and acting through it. Most of the students who chose puppetry did so because the troupe members were making puppets and they liked art. These students found satisfaction in performance only as a sequel to the puppet-making project. In a way they were taken totally by surprise as they never expected to perform.

Several different styles of puppetry—junk, plastic bottle, and shadow puppets as well as masks—were introduced to the group. Since students were not consistent in carrying out an idea, the variety enabled students to find some satisfaction in executing a work even in a short period. Because of their low self-esteem, it was important to choose a project from which there were immediate results to avoid reinforcing their feelings of failure.

The program began with a performance of the Underground Railway's show *Junk*, a comic fantasy satire on consumerism that features a combination of puppets, masks and actors. The students especially liked the humor of the show, and were receptive to it in great part because of its focus on a wealthy business man, a rod-puppet character. It was interesting to note that students who are so illiterate, traditionally speaking, are so savvy about the economy and their places in it, much more so than priviledged middle-income students.

The second half of the show featured puppets made from found objects or "junk." A workshop was held directly following the performance inviting students to make similar junk puppets from materials such as broken tools, battered umbrellas, utensils, and sponges that students and faculty previously assembled. Students were encouraged to bring in particular items that suggested personality characteristics and especially things with moving parts. The puppet building with objects was approached in an open ended and improvisational manner and only about one third of the group actually chose to participate in the puppet making. The remainder of the group stood at the sidelines, mostly pretending not to be interested and stray comments could be heard by students. One tough seventeen year old boy commented, "I hate art!" Whereas, a theater group member responded, "This isn't art, really. . ." (as a means to motivate the boy into further responses). The boy finally reciprocated with, "No? It's creative, ain't it."

The residency team at first was depressed when only ten puppets were produced by fifty students but were told by the staff that this was excellent. The students were very receptive. Clearly, the group had to revise its assessment of success in this project, looking at the environment and the student's history of learning.

Several problems were identified early in the project. Since students obviously had a hard time carrying out an idea, committing themselves to an idea's possibilities seemed scary. Perhaps they felt better throwing out many ideas and getting small amounts of reinforcement for each one. Maybe their lack of successful experiences made them afraid of carrying out a single idea and failing. For whatever reason, there was a lack of focus on a specific idea in puppet making. Students also found it difficult to preceive that their ideas were good when praised by staff members. Constant coaxing and encouragement was required to inch them far enough forward with a project so that they could see that it had certain promise.

Another stumbling block that progressed with puppet making was that many students were unfamiliar with materials and tools and felt helpless to use them. They required much assistance in these basic skills so often taken for granted with middle-income students.

In addition, the troupe members encountered demonstrations and feelings of self-hate which were illustrated through the students' lack of respect for their work. Students often destroyed what they or their peers made. Some of the nicest puppets were severly damaged while on display. But in spite of the problems involved, the group did end up with enough puppets to begin a puppet exhibit which was continued during the residency program at school. It turned out to be important that students' work could be seen and that they could show it off at anytime they wished. It made the project seem real.

Next the group moved on to creating rod and hand puppets. Again the troupe opted for simplicity and used everyday materials, this time plastic bottles of different shapes and sizes. A dowel was inserted inside these puppets to serve as a hand grip, and a cardboard shoulder yoke was attached to the neck of the bottle. A simple cloth costume draped over this yoke formed the basic costume. Yarn hair and odds and ends were used for features. The group was able to explore the wide range of characters that could be developed from this basic idea. A gypsy, several hip and streetwise types, and athletes were popular outcomes. One of the most interesting puppets was made

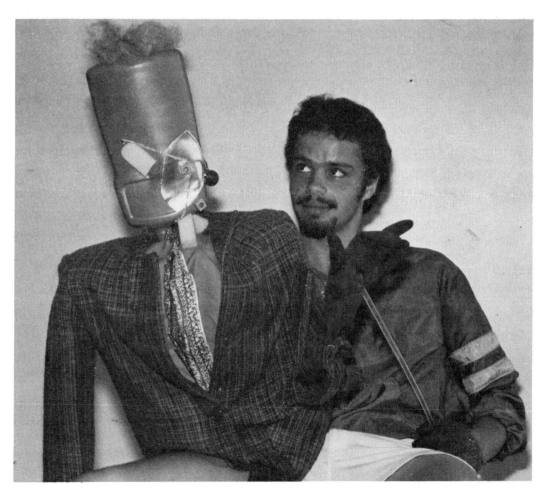

An unusual character from a "Puerto Rican Planet"—*Plastic Bottle Puppet—Photo by Lorenzo Deitch*

141

by a Puerto Rican student who exhibited his own feelings of cultural isolation when he explained that his unusual character covered with odd knobs and ornaments came from a "Puerto Rican planet." This student was one of the few Hispanics in a largely black school and often felt isolated. His puppet gave him opportunity to act out his feelings through comedy.

The bottle puppets were operated with one hand on the rod underneath the costume and the other hand sticking out of the sleeve or a hole in the costume to suggest the hand of the puppet. This was an easy method and close to the puppeteer's own gestures, an idea the troupe wished to capitalize on to make the process of performing less awkward or difficult to the students.

A third option for puppet making was offered in shadow puppetry. This puppetry technique utilizes cardboard shapes silhouetted against a semi-opaque screen with a light behind it that produces a magical effect in shadow which turned out to be perfect for sea themes, especially around the Boston Harbor. A fourth option offered students, although not puppets but related to puppetry, was masks which were made with plaster gauze using students' faces as forms. This method intrigued students as the results were quite beautiful and they enjoyed seeing the images of their own faces in the final masks. They also took turns trying on each other's masks which was great fun.

Formal performance with puppets was not actually attempted. Instead, students demonstrated them on an informal level at an event on the final day of the residency. Also, an improvisation was done with the creature from a "Puerto Rican Planet."

Nevertheless, the puppets did get a lot of play in the classroom, art room and hall. Students gravitated to these colorful characters and enjoyed them immensely as a whole. One particularly anti-social young man, distracted and violent when depressed, had created a quite beautiful puppet with practically no help. Immediately after completion, he took it out into the hall and it came to life as "The Puppet Man."

Another student who had been previously remote from the project, upon seeing the puppets displayed, began making cityscapes of Boston for a background for the puppets. He became fanatical about the scenes and worked on them every spare minute. Although he had drawn cities before, they never served a function such as on this occasion.

Summary of Project

The combined puppetry projects did succeed in taking the students outside themselves, to discover at least a tip of the wit, beauty, and creativity they possessed. Several were even amazed at themselves. Finally, all of those who did participate succeeded in creating something of beauty that others appreciated, a very rare experience for the students. Primarily, this project allowed students to get in touch with the child in themselves. Because of the toughness and depression of their neighborhoods, their families, the necessity for them to take on financial and family responsibilities, these students have had to "grow up" too fast. Their natural whimsy and wit is too early obscured by a need to be tough and self-sufficient. Puppetry gave them an opportunity to experience the parts of themselves—creativity, spontaneity, playfulness—they thought that they had to bury in order to get along.

It was extremely useful for these students to have visited the troupe's studio at one point in this learning experience to view how professional artists and performers work. The visit allowed them to understand that artists are serious adults engaged in play and that beautiful environments *can* be created without a great deal of money. Also, they realized that artists can make a living at art. It is hoped the entire experience will help make art more accessible to the students in the future and will undermine their notions that art isn't meant for them, that it is reserved for the more educated and elite. After all, these students have already experienced the process of being creators themselves!

Debra Wise is a member of the Underground Railway Puppets and Actors and had explored mask, mime, and actor's theatre in her work as a performer/teacher. Ms. Wise has studied puppetry/theatre in Poland, Germany, Belgium, and Holland. She has designed several innovative residency programs for disadvantaged populations during the past ten years. Debra has continued to explore how the arts and politics can be integrated into her work.

Edward M. Pazzanese is an experienced Community Arts organizer and teacher committed to developing cultural education programs for low income and disabled learners. He is currently the Director of the Exploratory Arts Program at Cambridge Camping Association and was a finalist for the Jon Anson Kittredge Awards—Harvard University School of Government in 1983—for his work in community arts education.

Special thanks to Richard Lewis, Roberta Kalinoski and Elizabeth Lee, for their support of this community work.

Students enjoyed seeing the images of their own faces in the final maskes—*Photo by Lorenzo Deitch*

RESOURCES

Books   In Paperback

Puppetry in Early Childhood Education by Tamara Hunt and Nancy Renfro. Comprehensive resource for "Puppetization" of hundreds of new learning activities. Preschool through Grade 3.

Puppetry and the Art of Story Creation by Nancy Renfro. Excellent guide on "how-to" create a story with many simple puppet ideas for an integrated curriculum approach. Special section on puppetry for the disabled.

A Puppet Corner in Every Library by Nancy Renfro. Superb step-by-step guide for incorporating puppetry into the library for storytelling, loan-bags and setting up a puppet corner.

Puppetry and Creative Dramatics in Storytelling by Connie Champlin, illustrated by Nancy Renfro. Imaginative puppetry and creative dramatics activities for group participation based on children's literature.

Make Amazing Puppets by Nancy Renfro and Beverly Armstrong. Jammed packed with exciting ideas for making puppets from paper products and recycled junk.

Puppet Shows Made Easy! by Nancy Renfro. Easy hints and how to for aspects of show productions.

An Exciting Series:

Pocketful of Puppets: Activities for the Special Child by Debbie Sullivan, illustrated by Nancy Renfro.

Pocketful of Puppets: Mother Goose Rhymes by Tamara Hunt and Nancy Renfro

Pocketful of Puppets: Three Plump Fish and Other Short Stories by Yvonne Winer, illustrated by Nancy Renfro.

Pocketful of Puppets: Poems for Church School by Lynn Irving, illustrated by Nancy Renfro

NANCY RENFRO STUDIOS
Special Media for the Special Child

In a bold move to make the art of puppetry accessible to all persons, Nancy Renfro Studios has developed a unique line of puppet media for the disabled. Included in the line are:

- **Discover the Super Senses through Puppetmime.** *A kit for the disabled that combines a versatile bodi-puppet with creative dramatics activities for allowing handicapped students to discover new language and curriculum potential. Also available are six additional kits, one for each handicapped area, in a special disability awareness program for non-handicapped students.*
- **Wheelchair stages** *that fit over standard wheelchairs.*
- **Puppet Bracelets** *for children with limited motor dexterity.*
- **Speech Pillow** *for tongue and teeth practice.*

Discover the Super Sense·
·Bodi Puppet

Write For Free Catalogue
Over 200 Puppet Characters•Show Kits•Books•Special Child

Nancy Renfro Studios
1117 W. 9th Street, Austin, Tx 78703
(512) 472-2140

Organizations

NATIONAL COMMITTEE • ARTS FOR THE HANDI-CAPPED—This superb organization has made widespread impact across the nation in accelerating the arts amongst the disabled population. They feature a regular newsletter with updates on grants and special arts festivals held in various locations. Write John F. Kennedy Center for the Performing Arts, Education Office, Washington DC 20566

PUPPETEERS OF AMERICA—National organization for the betterment of puppetry, with membership from many parts of the world. Offers an annual Puppet Festival; a Puppetry Store for purchasing books and puppet items; a bi-monthly magazine; consultant services and affiliated guilds located around the country. A small membership fee is required. Write for information about your local puppet guild. Puppeteers of America, Gayle C. Schluter, Treasurer, *#15 Cricklewood Path, Pasadena CA 91107*

NATIONAL STORYTELLING RESOURCE CENTER—An organization specializing in exploring and upgrading the quality of storytelling techniques. Annual storytelling convention as well as a comprehensive resource center. National Storytelling Resource Center, P.O. Box 112, Jonesborbough TN 37659

ONTARIO PUPPETRY ASSOCIATION—A Canadian puppetry organization offering various activities and services. Kenneth McKay, Executive Secretary, 10 Skyview Crescent, Willowdale, Ontario M2J 1B8, Canada

BRITISH PUPPET CENTRE—A British group offering various services. Write to: British Puppet Centre, Battersea Town Hall, Lavender Hill, London S.W. 11, England

KIDS ON THE BLOCK—A nationally known education group that has done outstanding work in developing programs to build awareness among the non-handicapped about the handicapped. They have available complete kits with puppets, manuals and activities on the six disabling categories plus other areas such as drug abuse. They also have a regular newsletter, **Kids on the Block**. 1712 Eye Street N.W. Suite 1008, Washington DC 20006

Puppet Manufacturers

The following represents a wide assortment of puppet manufacturers across the country. Some of the companies sell wholesale and retail; others sell only wholesale requiring a minimum order ranging from $100 to $200. By writing for a free catalogue each company will forward its individual ordering policies and catalogue.

CLOTH CREATURES—A finely crafted line of adoring furry creatures with talking mouths. Of special interest is the Little People Lap Puppet (3 feet tall). Also makes custom puppets to order. Cloth Creatures, 281 E. Millan Street, Chula Vista, CA 92010

CHILD GUIDANCE—This toy company puts out a line of the famed Sesame Street puppets in both hand and finger-puppet types. Child Guidance, 41 Madison Ave. New York 10011

DAKIN & COMPANY—This well-known toy company has an extensive line of hand puppets and plush toys from an array of soft, cuddly fabrics, including most popular animals. Dakin, P.O. Box 7746, Rincon Annex, San Francisco, CA 94120

DOT DAWN—Sells a variety of puppet lines, retail, including Dakin, Furry Folks and a particularly lovable line of animals with super long arms for hugging. Dot Dawn, 324 County Line Road, Griffin GA 30223

DRAGONS ARE TOO SELDOM—Has a line of talking mouth hand puppets, some people, animals (Disco Duck, Abbey Deer and Lambie) and fantasy types. Dragons Are Too Seldom, 649 Main Street, Deadwood SD 57732

FURRY FOLKS PUPPETS—Offers a selection of 23 cuddly furry wildlife creatures some of which have baby offspring. Includes bears, seals, rabbits, squirrels and other woodland friends. Furry Folks Puppets, 1219 Park Avenue, Emeryville CA 94608

HAPPY HOLLOW PUPPETS—Creates customized puppets, mascot puppets, and entire show kits to order as well as offering a standard line of popular fairy tale characters with cassettes and scenery sets. Happy Hollow Puppets, 324 Zorn Ave., Louisville KY 40206

KIDS—Specializes in puppets and other media for the disabled such as finger puppets, coloring books and games. Kids, Whittier School, 1645 Milvia Street, Berkeley, CA 94709

L.K. HECHT CO., INC—Specializes in a line of finger puppets. L.K. Hecht Company, Inc., 1140 Broadway, New York NY 10001

LESWING PRESS—Kits for building reading, motor and speech skills. Includes a selection of hand and finger puppets for basic people, animals and fairy tales. Also carries Boris, Morris and Denny—large furry creatures. Leswing Press, P.O. Box 3577, San Rafael CA 94901

LOLLY RUZOTARSKI—Features a "Dancing Bear" puppet kit with finger puppets and interchangeable fairy tale scripts. Also carries soft sculpture body puppets and hand and rod puppets. Lolly Ruzotarski, 2019 N. Newhall Street, Milwaukee WI 53202

MARY MEYER MFG. CO, INC.—Offers a large selection of stuffed toys and 36 hand puppet characters of basic people and animals. Included are community workers, hobo, Indian, football player, owl and monkey. Mary Meyer Mfg. Co., Townshend, VT 05353

NANCY RENFRO STUDIOS—Offers over 300 puppet characters! For use in storytelling, show production, library, special child and early childhood. All puppets are washable, durable and handcrafted. Includes almost every type of animal (gerbil, octopus, platypus, anteater, polar bear, shark, donkey are a few examples); Holiday and fairy tale characters; people puppets of varied flesh tones; show puppets with matching cassettes and scripts; and puppets designed for the special child. Nancy Renfro Studios 1117 W. 9th Street, Austin TX 78703

PAKALUK PUPPETS—Stocks a colorful, well-designed line of hand puppets featuring most popular animals (with cute talking sock mouths) and basic people (Mexican, pirate, cowboy, fairy tale, etc.) Features large rod action puppets and a small sock puppet line that is especially appealing. Write to Pakaluk P.O. Box 129, Frederricksburg, TX 78624.

PLAYFUL PUPPETS, INC.—Carries a line of people puppets (in varied flesh tones) and numerous animal puppets (Booble Bird, Snider Spider and Thekla Turtle) with talking mouths. Playful Puppets, Inc. 4463 Charter Point Blvd. Jacksonville, FL 32211

POPPETS—Features a colorful doorway theater with a selection of 18 talking mouth, hand puppet characters. Includes royalty, medical, clown, ant, elf, animals and people. Poppets, 1800 E. Olive Way, Seattle WA 98102

REEVES INTERNATIONAL, INC.—Carries the famous German-made "Steiff" and "Kersa" brand puppets. Reeves International, Inc., 1107 Broadway, New York NY 10010

RUSHTON—Stocks a wide range of stuffed toys and puppets made from soft, cuddly fur fabrics. Also carries a nice line of crocheted puppets and stuffed food characters. Write for local distributor: Rushton, 1275 Ellsworth Industrial Drive NW, Atlanta GA 30325

TOUCH TOYS: Although not puppets these marvelous handcrafted stuffed toys were designed to give tactile joy to blind students and may easily be adapted as puppets. Touch Toy. 3519 Porter St. N.W., Washington DC 20016

Craft Suppliers

ZIMS—This mail order craft supply company sells retail all types of items, plastic eyes, glue, trims, pipe cleaners, etc. There is a four dollar charge (refundable upon first order of $20 or more) for a comprehensive book on all their items of excellent value to the ardent puppetmaker. Write to: Zim's P.O. Box 7620, Salt Lake City, UT 84107

Stages and Equipment

PUPPET HARDWARE—Offers excellent stages to libraries, puppeteers and schools. Features portable and collapsible types as well as custom to individual needs. Constructed from steel piping. Puppet Hardware, 730 Ecton Road, Akron OH 44304

GAYLORD BROS., INC.—Markets a lightweight, plastic corrugated small stage with window opening, ideal for a Puppet Corner or informal table-top performances. Order –L 104, Cost: $23.00. Write to: Gaylord Bros. Inc., Box 61, Syracuse NY 13201

POPPETS—Features a colorful hanging doorway fabric stage. Poppets, 1800 E. Olive Way, Seattle WA 98102

Recording

THE KING STREET RECORDING COMPANY—Offers custom recording, editing and duplication of tapes, cassettes, and 8-track cartridges. Poor recordings can be improved, and damaged recordings repaired. Complete sound tracks with voices, music and sound effects can be created for plays, puppet shows and audio-visual presentations. Write or call: The King Street Recording Company. P.O. Box 402, Malvern PA 19355 (215) 647-4341.

Books on Puppetry

The following list of books is taken from an annotated list (condensed version) compiled by the Puppeteer's of America Bookstore. Send $1.00 for their complete catalogue listing of books and prices. The Puppetry Store, 615 N. Bristol #90, Santa Ana, CA 92703.

ABC Puppetry, Vicki Rutter—A good reference book for the beginner. Information on making different types of puppets and stages. 77p. $5.95

The Art of Making Puppets and Marionettes, Charlene Davis Roth—Covering finger puppets, hand puppets, ventriloquist's figures, and marionettes. Three short plays are also included. 198 p. pap. $6.95

The Art of the Puppet, Bil Baird—A record of puppets throughout the ages, covering all forms and types from all sections of the globe. 251 p. $19.95

Books, Puppets and the Mentally Retarded Student, John and Connie Champlin—A unique book on cleverly integrating puppets and children's literature with the mentally retarded. 162 p. pap. $8.95

Bring on the Puppets. Helen Ferguson—Simple puppets for use in church or school teaching, including patterns. Six plays using various kinds of puppets, among them "The Christmas Story" and "The Story of Hannukkah." 31 p. pap. $3.25

Creative Puppets in the Classroom, Mary Freericks with Joyce Segal—Shows how to bring spontaneity to the classroom through the use of puppets. Instructions are given for making imaginative puppets from inexpensive materials and it includes techniques for incorporating puppets into the curriculum. 144 p. pap. $5.95

The Dwiggins Marionettes, Dorothy Abbe—A comprehensive record of one man's experiments with the marionette puppet theatre. A large, beautiful book and a rich experience for the reader. 232 p. $29.95

Easy To Make Puppets, Frieda Gates—The appeal is to the very young would-be puppeteer. Clearly illustrated with many patterns for hand, hand and rod, simple marionettes, and shadow puppets.

Easy To Make Puppets, Joyce Luckin—Over 20 puppets, mostly made of felt, are described. Both hand puppets and marionettes are shown, and one play is included. 47 p. $8.95

Easy To Make Puppets and How To Use Them: Early Childhood, Fran Rottman—Written for those who work with children 2 to 5 years of age, with emphasis on the use of puppets in the church, vacation Bible school, day camps, clubs, etc. Many patterns and illustrations. 96 p. pap. $3.95

Easy To Make Puppets and How To Use Them: Children & Youth, Fram Rottman—Emphasis is the same as in the book mentioned above, except with children of an older age group. 96 p. pap. $3.95

Eight Plays For Hand Puppets, edited by A.R. Philpott—Written by members of The Educational Puppetry Association in England. They are royalty-free and include such plays as "Punch and the Heartless Giant," "The Gingerbread Boy" and several original plays. 94 p. $7.95

Expert Puppet Technique, Eric Bramall and Christopher Somerville—A manual of production for puppeteers by two master puppet showmen, discussing scenic and puppet design, lighting, sound, movement, manipulation, writing plays and conducting rehearsals. 104 p. $7.95.

Folding Paper Puppets, Shari Lewis and Lillian Oppenheimer—The techniques of Origami—the Japanese art of paperfolding, illustrated with clear step-by-step instructions. 90 p. pap. $2.95

Folk Puppet Plays For the Social Studies, Margaret Weeks Adair and Elizabeth Patapoff—Sixteen puppet plays suitable for schoolroom production have been adapted from American and other ethnic tales. 120 p. $12.50

The Funcraft Book of Puppets, Violet Philpott and Mary Jean McNeil—Contains different ideas for "easy-to-make" puppets most of which could be made by an older child. Tips for staging, scenery, and sound effects are included. 45 p. pap. $2.95

Give Puppets a Hand, Violet Whittaker—A wide variety of scripts and includes basic instructions with illustrations and patterns, on how to get started in a puppet ministry. 104 p. pap. $4.95

Holiday Plays For Puppets or People, Eleanor Boylan—Contains thirteen plays which include Aesop's fables, well-known fairy tales, original plays and Punch and Judy. 93 p. pap. $4.00

Learning With Puppets, Hans J. Schmidt and Karl J. Schmidt—A guide to making and using puppets in the classroom. Stresses ways to enhance individual artistic expression and the acquisition of social and academic skills. 85 p. pap. $6.95

Learning With Puppets. David Currell—Technical directions are given for making all types of puppets. An excellent reference book for those past the stage of "easy-to-make," as well as those involved in education. 205 p. $15.95

The Magic of Puppetry: A Guide for Those Working with Young Children, Peggy Davison Jenkins—Aimed primarily at children 3 to 9 years old and has information on instant puppets, simple stages and manipulation. 142 p. pap. $5.95

Make Amazing Puppets, Nancy Renfro and Beverly Armstrong—Lots of very clever, easy-to-make puppets. All could be made by children and the clear drawings show the supplies needed, many different types and variations of these types. Some of the ideas given include trick puppets, puppets you can wear, cardboard marionettes and ways to stretch your imagination! 32 p. pap. $4.95

Making Glove Puppets, Esme McLaren—Many full size patterns (mostly animals). Includes full instructions on cutting and sewing the puppet, and on designing clothes and accessories. 218 p. $12.95

Making Puppets Come Alive, Larry Engler and Carol Fijan —A must for those learning manipulation with hand puppets. A method of learning and teaching hand puppetry, which has been called "The Stanislavsky of the hand puppet world." Good puppet theatrical technique, including voice use, improvisation, role characterization and other fundamental elements are covered. 191 p. $9.95

Marionettes on Stage, Leonard Suib and Muriel Broadman —The book is divided into three major parts: "The New Marionette;" "Becoming a Puppeteer;" and "Puppet Theater Management." 243 p. 83 line drawings. 33 photos $16.95

Mime and Masks, Roberta Nobelman—Varieties of mime and techniques for making them work are offered along with ways to use masks. Five scenarios of mime and mask plays. 152 p. pap. $5.95

Modern Puppetry, A.R. Philpott—The making and operating of many kinds of puppets are covered with in-depth sections on characterization, shadow puppets, plasticine heads, rod puppets and marionettes. 128 p. $7.95

More Practical Puppet Plays, Irvy Gilbertson—Contains 17 puppet scripts to be used for children to teach everyday applications of Bible Scripture. 64 p. pap. $2.50

More Puppets with Pizazz, Joy Wilt and Gwen and John Hurn—50 ideas for rod, novelty and string puppets children can make and use. Includes patterns. 159 p. pap. $5.95

Needlework Puppets, Brenda Morton—A detailed pattern and instruction book for the making of some twenty hand puppets. 136 p. $6.95

Pint Sized Puppet Projects, Beverly Armstrong—24 Spirit duplication masters to make quickie stick and finger puppets. $5.50

Paper-Bag Puppets, Deatna Williams.—There are 48 easy character patterns to color and use with paper bag puppets including animal and holiday characters. $5.50

More Paper-Bag Puppets, Deatna Williams—A sequel to above book includes patterns for community workers, fairy tales and seasonal characters. $5.50

Plays for Puppet Performance, George Merten—Ten original scripts of puppet plays which can be performed with hand puppets or marionettes. 90 p. $9.95

Pocketful of Puppets Series, by Nancy Renfro Studios. A great series and expanding series: **Mother Goose** $7.50; **Three Plump Fish and Other Short Stories** $6.50; **Poems for Church School** $6.50; and **Activities for the Special Child** $6.50

Practical Puppet Plays, by Irvy Gilbertson—17 short scripts for children ages 2-12 which include a Bible reference. 61 p. pap. $2.50

The Puppet Book, Wall, White and Philpott—Discusses all forms of puppetry, all types of construction, plus chapters on plays and production. A couple of short hand puppet plays are included. 300 p. $9.95

The Puppet People, Pat Zabriskie—17 short skits in this book are all based on Bible truths and could be used for Sunday Schools or Vacation Bible Schools. 63 p. pap. $2.95

Puppet Shows That Reach and Teach Children, Joyce Reynolds—For teachers who want to present Bible truths using puppetry. Each volume includes 10 hand puppet stories, handcraft projects and a puppet theater pattern. pap.

*Vol. 1 Parables of Jesus	$2.95
*Vol. 2 Life of Jesus	$3.50
*Vol. 3 Book of Acts	$3.50

Puppet Stages and Props with Pizzaz, Joy Wilt and Gwen and John Hurn—Very interesting ways to make simple stages and props for or with children. Lighting and simple puppet costumes are also explained. 140 p. pap.

Puppetry and Creative Dramatics in Storytelling, Connie Champlin—Simple puppetry and creative dramatics are used to bring storytelling sessions to life. Ideas are given for group participation based on traditional and modern children's stories. Teachers, librarians or storytellers can use the suggestions for sound effects, music, action and pantomime with children from pre-school to 12 years old. 132 p. pap.

Puppetry and the Art of Story Creation, Nancy Renfro—This book is full of wonderful ideas for creating a story to be used with puppets. There are original and clever ideas for simple puppets along with a very complete list of sources of material and information. The section on puppetry for the special child includes those who are physically disabled as well as those who are hearing and visually impaired. 166 p. pap.

Puppetry and Early Childhood Education, Tamara Hunt and Nancy Renfro. It is jam-packed with all kinds of creative and stimulating puppet ideas that can be used with children up to third grade. Holiday, curriculum, songs, self-concepts are just a few areas covered.

Puppetry for School Children, David Currell—The sections include: Why do puppetry? Writing the script; Hand, Sock and Rod puppets; The Marionette; a Simple Stage and much more. 80 p.

Puppetry In Canada—An Art To Enchant, Kenneths B. McKay—An authoritative study of contemporary Canadian puppetry and it is illustrated with over 80 large, clear black and white photographs of the work of leading Canadian puppeteers. 168 p.

Puppetry In The Teaching of Foreign Language, Mary Nadjar Weinstein—Teaching and learning of foreign languages is a performing art. Theory is explained in the first section and the remainder of the book is devoted to "Three French Workshops on Stage," each of which contains a small play or dialogue. 38 p.

Puppetry, The Ultimate Disguise, George Latshaw—Many aspects of the puppet theatre are discussed, including design, voices and sound effects, characterization, stages and playwriting. Excellent for older students and college level puppetry. 158 p.

Puppets and Therapy, edited by A.R. Philpott—Brings together innovative ideas and experiments for the use of puppets and puppetry with the physically handicapped and the emotionally and mentally impaired. 153 p.

Puppets For All Grades, Scott, May and Shaw—Various types of puppets constructed from simple materials. Very useful for teachers. Class projects made easy. 48 p. pap.

Puppets For Beginners, Moritz Jagendorf—Imaginative and colorful pictures help beginners create and use hand puppets and marionettes, make the stage and costumes. Recommended for ages 7-12. 68 p

Puppets For the Classroom, Alison Vandergun—Puppets are designed to be quick and simple to make, and easy to teach. A loose folded sheet of patterns is included. 34 p. pap.

Puppets From Polyfoam: Sponge-Ees, Bruce Chesse and Beverly Armstrong—Special emphasis on construction, this book features guidelines for using polyfoam to construct quick and interesting hand puppets with glue or staple gun. Good for the young and the adult puppeteer. 37 p. pap.

Puppets Go To Church, Earl and Wilma Perry—Gives the "How-To's" of puppetry and then shares nineteen scripts which the authors have used with their handmade puppets and screens. 87 p. pap.

Puppets in Phonics and Reading, Charlotte Kohrs—The book's subtitle, "Nine ways to use puppets to build language skills and confidence" gives the purpose of the book. This is achieved through selected sounds, phrases and sentences incorporated into easy "I read/You read" dialogues, choral verse, and puppet plays. 83 p. pap. $3.50

Puppets With a Purpose, K.F. Hughes—Ideas, patterns and activities are given for many simple puppets made from easily found materials. Great ideas for those who work with children. 23 p. pap. $2.00

Puppets With Pizzaz, Joy Wilt and Gwen and John Hurn—52 Finger and Hand puppets children can make and use. 159 p. pap. $5.95

A Puppet Corner In Every Library, Nancy Renfro—Librarians everywhere are realizing that there is something quite extraordinary about puppets and that children's services can benefit from their use. A puppet on the hand of a sensitive person becomes an invaluable tool of communication, and on the hand of child, an extension of his thoughts and feelings. Contains pictures, patterns, articles and resource list. 110 p. pap. $9.95

Puppet Making Through The Grades, Grideila Hopper—A book for young people, teachers, and others who work with children. Paper bags, boxes, socks, balloons, styrofoam and many other everyday items combine to form appealing puppets. 64 p. $6.95

Puppet Plays For Young Players, Lewis Mahlmann and David Cadwalader Jones—Twelve fast-paced scripts include original plays, adaptations, dramatizations, even spoofs on familiar fairy tales, legends and classics. 194 p. $9.95

Puppet Plays From Favorite Stories, Lewis Mahlmann and David Cadwalader Jones—A collection of 18 one-act, royalty-free puppet plays adapted from famous stories and fairy tales for production by young people. 204 p. $9.95

Puppet Scripts For Children's Church, Jessie P. Sullivan—In these scripts, Mortimer and Mathilda Puppet teach each other (and their audience) Bible verses, and apply Bible truths to the everyday situations children frequently encounter. 111 p. pap. $2.95

Puppet Stages and Props with Pizazz, Joy Wilt and Gwen and John Hurn—Easy to make stages of all sorts made from boxes, chairs, etc. Also ideas for simple props and costuming. $5.95

Puppet Theatre Handbook, Marjorie Batchelder—Covers practically every phase of puppet construction and production, bringing together contributions of technical knowledge from more than 50 outstanding puppeteers. Includes bibliography and materials supplement. 293 p. $9.95.

The Puppet Theatre In America, Paul McPharlin, supplement by Marjorie McPharlin—An authentic and complete history of the growth of the puppet art in America. Many rare and unusual prints in the original text. 734 p. $13.95

Puppet Theatre in Performance, Nancy H. Cole—A valuable book for anyone interested in puppetry. In addition to giving a lively history of puppet theatre, it covers pertinent topics for adapting the essential theatre arts to the special needs of the puppet theatre. 272 p. $14.95

Putting It All Together In a Puppet Ministry, Fredda Marsh—This "how-to" manual tells how to present plays for children and organize a puppet ministry in your church. There are about 20 scripts based on Bible truths, each of which lasts 5 minutes. 144 p. pap. $6.95

Shadow Images Of Asia, Bettie Erda—A selection of shadow puppets from The American Museum of Natural History are shown from China, India, Thailand, Malaysia, Java and Bali. 47 p. pap. $4.00

Shadow Plays, Edited by Betsy Stott—Directions are given for performing four authentic Asian shadow plays from China, India, Java and Thailand. Also included are directions for making shadow puppets and a simple shadow screen. 20 p. pap. $1.50

Shadow Puppetry For the Church School, Elain Carlson—Complete patterns and instructions for presenting four Bible stories with shadow puppets. Scripts are included for "The Birth of Jesus," "The Sower and the Seed," "The Good Samaritan," and "Jesus Beside the Sea." 24 oversize p. pap. $2.95

Shadow Puppetry on the Overhead Projector, Janibeth Johnson—A detailed, technical and somewhat complex description of this type of projection of shadow images that approach the quality of animated film. Many helpful tips on making shadow puppets and an invaluable list of equipment and materials. 20 p. $3.75

Shadow Puppets in Color, Louise Cochrane—For the beginner in shadow puppetry. Diagrams, patterns, and directions for staging and musical effects. Three shadow plays are included. A Chinese legend, a play from the Greek shadow theater, and a Hindu-Japanese legend. 48 p. $5.95

Shadow Puppets, Shadow Theatres and Shadow Films, Lotte Reiniger—The most complete book on shadow puppetry available. Describes the history of shadow theater, how to produce shadow shows and films, including animation, photography and synchronizaiton of the sound track. 28 p. $10.00

Sir George's Book of Hand Pupppetry, George Creegan—For the beginning puppeteer. directions for making and manipulating hand puppets and rod puppets. Contains his adaptations of the play, "The Night It Rained Toys." 94 p. pap. $2.98

Space Age Puppets and Masks, M.C. Green and B.R.H. Targett—An up-to-date emphasis on puppet making for the older child. This book is useful for home or school as the puppets are made from easily found objects. $7.95

Teaching Bible Stories More Effectively With Puppets, Roland Sylwester—Step-by-step instructions for simple to more advanced hand puppets, shadow puppets, and marionettes, as well as twelve Bible story-based scripts with stage direction. 64 p. pap. $2.50

Ventriloquism, Darryl Hutton—For the beginning ventriloquist. "How to put on an act, use the power of suggestion, and make your own dummy." 128 p. $6.95

The Voices and Hands of Bunraku, Barbara Curtis Adachi—Deals with people of Bunraku—the narrators, the musicians, the puppeteers, and the unseen others, who carry on this highly developed puppet drama, a three hundred year old art. 148 p. $19.95

Wood Spoon Puppets, Audrey Vincente Dean—Using wooden spoons for the construction of puppets. Detailed, well illustrated instructions are given for making twelve puppets, a simple stage, and two short plays. 92 p. $10.95

Pamphlets

Puppetry in the Classroom, Carol Sterling—This manual will help teachers use puppets for creative expression and curriculum development. 35 p. $1.00

Puppetry Workshop Manual, Conrad R. Woyce—Actual size patterns for making several types of hand puppets, animal puppets, mouth (or Muppet)-type puppets, rod puppets and marionettes. 28 p. patterns. $4.50

Puppets For Schools, Coad Canada Puppets—Provides teachers with instructions for making a wide range of functional puppets from materials that are reasonably easy to obtain and simple to handle. Includes diagrams and patterns. 20 p. $2.50

Script-Writing Workbook, Judy Brown—This workbook lets you write a puppet play for any type of puppet from your own imagination. A series of questions along with your own answers leads you from the first idea through style, characterization, action and dialogue. 25 p. $4.00

Start With A Balloon, R.C. (Nick) LeFeuvre—A step-by-step explanation of the method used in making puppet heads using a balloon as a base, each step clearly and fully illustrated. 12 p. $.65

Using Puppets in Schools, Coad Canada Puppets—The emphasis in this publication is on the effective use of hand puppets in a school situation rather than on puppet construction. Exercises to strengthen the puppeteers' hands, suggestions for voice, for characterization and for improvement of all phases of hand puppet manipulation. 16 p. $3.00